Norms in International Relations

A volume in the series

Cornell Studies in Political Economy

EDITED BY PETER J. KATZENSTEIN

A full list of titles in the series appears at the end of the book.

Norms in International Relations

THE STRUGGLE AGAINST APARTHEID

AUDIE KLOTZ

CORNELL UNIVERSITY PRESS

Ithaca and London

First published 1995 by Cornell University Press.

Printed in the United States of America

⊗ The paper in this book meets the minimum requirements of the American National Standard for Information Sciences—Permanence of Paper for Printed Library Materials, ANSI Z39.48-1984.

Library of Congress Cataloging-in-Publication Data

Klotz, Audie, b. 1962
    Norms in international relations : The struggle against apartheid
/ Audie Klotz.
        p.   cm.
    Includes bibliographical references and index.
    ISBN 0-8014-3106-9 (cloth : alk. paper)
    1. Apartheid—South Africa. 2. South Africa—Relations—Foreign
countries.   I. Title.
DT1757.K55   1995
305.8'00968—dc20   95-19361

In memory of Maria Askounis

Contents

Acknowledgments

For international relations theorists, 1989 marked the end of bi-polarity and the demise of communism. But 1989 was also the year of Namibian independence and the "purple rain" demonstrations in South Africa, and we impatiently awaited the (rumored) release of Nelson Mandela. Although this book is firmly rooted in southern Africa, I have chosen to privilege questions about international relations. I hope Africans and Africanists will also discover space in international relations theory for their intellectual and practical concerns.

Some exceptionally sympathetic people have enabled me to totter along the dividing line between international and African politics. Peter Katzenstein and Locksley Edmondson signed on to a project that took each of them through unknown territory; they offered invaluable comments throughout the subsequent years. I have also benefited immensely from discussions with and comments from colleagues too numerous to list individually, especially at Cornell University, Yale University, the Institute of Commonwealth Studies at the University of London, the University of Zimbabwe, and the University of Southern California. My students at Haverford College and the University of Illinois at Chicago helped me to clarify the essence of my arguments; for their patience and enthusiasm I am most grateful.

Graduate fellowships from the National Science Foundation and the MacArthur Program on International Peace and Security at the Social Science Research Council made my research travels possible, and friends on three continents gave me perspective. The Center for International Studies at the University of Southern California funded invaluable time to rethink and rewrite, and Roger Haydon patiently provided tutorials on the publication process. Chapters 2 and 6 contain material first published in my "Norms Reconstituting Interests: Global Racial Equality and U.S. Sanctions against South Africa," *International Organization* 49 (Summer 1995), with permission of the IO Foundation and MIT Press. In chapters 8 and 10, I have used modified portions of my "Race and Nationalism in Zimbabwean Foreign Policy," *The Round Table* 327 (July 1993), 255–79, with permission of the publisher, The Round Table Ltd.

For their essential encouragement and insightful criticism along the way, I owe special thanks to Dave Black, Eileen Crumm, Paul D'Anieri, Christine Ingebritsen, Anita Isaacs, Chris Reus-Smit, Thomas Risse-Kappen, Cherie Steele, and Alex Wendt. Most of all, I am indebted to Peter Katzenstein for being a friend to me and to this project—without his patience and generosity, I would have quit long ago. I only hope the final product is worth their investment.

This book is dedicated to my maternal grandmother, who influenced my life and this project in more ways than she ever would have imagined.

A. K.

Chicago
July 1994

Abbreviations

ANC	African National Congress
CBC	Congressional Black Caucus
CZI	Confederation of Zimbabwean Industries
EEC	European Economic Community
EPG	Eminent Persons Group
FLS	Frontline States
NAACP	National Association for the Advancement of Colored People
OAU	Organization of African Unity
SADCC	Southern African Development Coordination Conference
UDI	Unilateral Declaration of Independence
UKSATA	United Kingdom–South Africa Trade Association
ZANU	Zimbabwean African National Union
ZAPU	Zimbabwean African People's Union

PART I

OVERVIEW

Chapter One

The International Politics
of Apartheid

On 10 May 1994, the world celebrated Nelson Mandela's inauguration as the first democratically elected president of South Africa. After decades of protest, imprisonment, and exile, anti-apartheid activists achieved their goal of universal suffrage, eliminating the last vestige of white minority rule in Africa. After decades of fearing violent revolution and communist expansion, the Afrikaner-dominated National Party peacefully negotiated itself out of power. Domestic and international pressures to end apartheid had succeeded.[1]

So much global attention on the domestic politics of another country—either celebrating democratic elections or condemning racial discrimination—is unusual in a world of sovereign states, and global anti-apartheid sanctions demonstrate an even more extraordinary consensus on policy. By 1986 all of South Africa's major trading partners had implemented some form of international economic sanctions. In an unusual display of initiative, the U.S. Congress passed a sanctions package despite the objections of the Reagan administration. Even the Conservative Thatcher government in Britain, long seen as South Africa's

---

1. Leonard Thompson succinctly summarizes South African apartheid, translated from Afrikaans as "separateness" or "separate development," as a plethora of laws and executive actions that propagated four central ideas: (1) four "racial groups," Whites, Coloureds, Asians, and Africans (each with its own inherent culture), make up the country's population; (2) whites are entitled to absolute control over the state because they are the "civilized race"; (3) white interests prevail over black interests; and (4) whites constitute one race, despite differences between Afrikaans and English speakers, whereas Africans belong to several distinct nations. See his *A History of South Africa* (New Haven: Yale University Press, 1990), p. 190.

most stalwart Western ally, agreed to Commonwealth and European Community voluntary "measures" restricting trade with South Africa. Responding to earlier calls for sanctions, Japan had already restricted direct investment in 1968; later, following U.S. policy, it adopted trade restrictions in 1985 and 1986. These international sanctions against apartheid are particularly puzzling for international relations theories that emphasize the difficulties of coordinating multilateral policies and the primacy of material interests.

Because South Africa institutionalized segregation at a time when the international trend was to favor racial equality, this global reaction to domestic discrimination reflected the exceptional nature of apartheid policies. Indeed, as international criticism of apartheid increased, the South African government tried to justify its segregation in cultural rather than racial terms. In attempting to establish the nominal independence of its rural African reserves, or "tribal homelands," South Africa proclaimed that it did not exclude Africans from political participation because they were enfranchised in these supposedly sovereign states. Although the racial and cultural dimensions coexisted uneasily, the Afrikaner ideology of apartheid privileged group (rather than individual) rights. Even after the official demise of apartheid in the early 1990s, conservative Afrikaners continued to demand cultural autonomy in an independent white *volkstaat* (people's state), fueling demands for a decentralized or federal government.[2] Thus the white minority fundamentally rejected global demands for a political system based primarily on individual rights.

The illegitimacy of white minority rule led to South Africa's persistent diplomatic, cultural, and economic isolation. Only South African reforms begun in 1990 mitigated international condemnation, and only a constitutional system based on universal suffrage in 1994 ensured the end of the country's isolation. But objections to apartheid were long-standing—many opponents of apartheid adopted sanctions in the 1950s and 1960s—and the wide-ranging acceptance of economic restrictions by 1986 cannot be explained merely as the result of

2. Most Africans had never seen the areas that the government proclaimed to be their homes. No state other than South Africa recognized these homelands as sovereign states. On the homelands policies, see Thompson, *History of South Africa*, chap. 6. On ethnicity and apartheid, see contributions in *The Creation of Tribalism in Southern Africa*, ed. Leroy Vail (Berkeley: University of California Press, 1991). For a more detailed explanation of group rights and constitutional demands, see Donald L. Horowitz, *A Democratic South Africa? Constitutional Engineering in a Divided Society* (Berkeley: University of California Press, 1991).

4

Table 1. Sanctions against South Africa, 1960–1989

	Military[a]	Trade[b]	Finance[c]
MULTILATERAL			
UN General Assembly	1962–63, 1983	1962, 1965	1966, 1969
UN Security Council	1977, 1984	1985 voluntary	1985 voluntary
Commonwealth	1971	1985–86	1985–86
European Community	1985	1986	1986
Nordic countries	1977, 1985	1985–87	1979, 1985–86
Organization of African Unity	1963	1963	1963
BILATERAL .			
United States	1963, 1977, 1985, 1986	1978, 1985–86	1985–86
Britain	1985	1986	1985–87
West Germany	1986	1977	1977 informal
France	1985–86	1986	1985
Japan	1986	1986 informal	1969, 1985–86

Source: Based on summaries in Timothy M. Mozia, "Chronology of Arms Embargoes against South Africa" and "Chronology of Economic Embargoes against South Africa," in *Effective Sanctions on South Africa: The Cutting Edge of Economic Intervention,* ed. George W. Shepherd, Jr. (Westport, Conn.: Greenwood Press, 1991), pp. 97–108 and 108–25; and *South Africa: The Sanctions Report, Documents and Statistics,* ed. Joseph Hanlon (London: James Currey, 1990).

Note: Dates indicate only initiation of substantive new measures.

[a]Including oil and technology in addition to arms.

[b]Including airline landing rights in addition to imports and exports.

[c]Including Krugerrands in addition to investments, loans, and credits.

a sudden awareness of apartheid. Despite world condemnation after both the 1960 Sharpeville and 1976 Soweto uprisings, the West refused to adopt sanctions before the 1980s. Illustrating the contrasts in reactions between Western countries and those of early apartheid opponents, Table 1 summarizes the timing of major sanctions against South Africa.[3]

However, since no state conforms to international norms in all aspects of its domestic or foreign policies, we cannot say that South Africa's defiance of an international norm of racial equality, in and of itself, caused its international isolation. Only certain states become the

3. Apartheid opponents controlled the UN General Assembly and the Organization of African Unity. In addition (not listed in Table 1), India stopped trading with South Africa in 1946 and cut diplomatic ties in 1956. Other apartheid opponents, including the Soviet Union, Eastern European countries, and many African states cut economic ties in the 1960s. For the most comprehensive survey of sanctions against South Africa see Deon Geldenhuys, *Isolated States: A Comparative Analysis* (Cambridge: Cambridge University Press, 1990).

targets of sanctions intended to enforce compliance, and even fewer become "pariah states." To understand sanctions against South Africa and the enforcement of a global norm of racial equality, therefore, we need to examine how the loose coalition of governments, nongovernmental organizations, and individuals that made up the transnational anti-apartheid movement globalized concern over domestic discrimination.

By actively advocating a norm of racial equality and consequently altering the agendas of international organizations and the interests of states, the anti-apartheid movement successfully challenged South Africa's defensive claim to domestic jurisdiction and the mainstream policy consensus that sanctions do not work. After domestic unrest in South Africa flared in 1984 (following constitutional reforms in 1983 that granted political rights to Indians and Coloureds but not Africans), even South Africa's most loyal allies adopted sanctions to signal support for racial equality. What remains to be explained is how and why this consensus around racial equality, evident in global discourse by the mid-1960s, translated into sanctions policies in the mid-1980s.

The increasing strength of a global norm of racial equality— achieved through the efforts of advocates including the anti-apartheid movement—provides a systematic though preliminary explanation of the adoption of sanctions against South Africa by a broad and diverse range of international organizations and states. Yet our understanding of the relationship between norms and sanctions, both in this particular case and more generally, remains limited.[4] Consequently, analyzing the success of anti-apartheid sanctions, in terms both of the extraordinary degree of international coordination and of influencing South African domestic reform, will enhance our understanding of when and why

4. Few analytical studies of international sanctions examine the role of norms. Geldenhuys's *Isolated States* identifies abrogation of norms as important but does not pursue its analytical significance. Kim Richard Nossal argues that sanctions are sometimes used punitively to express moral disapproval but assumes rather than explains the role of norms; see his "International Sanctions as International Punishment," *International Organization* 43 (Spring 1989), 301–22. Lisa L. Martin, in *Coercive Cooperation: Explaining Multilateral Economic Sanctions* (Princeton: Princeton University Press, 1992), analyzes the role of institutions in coordinating sanctions policies but does not examine the abrogation of norms as a motivation for sanctions. Rather, she subsumes the reasons for adopting sanctions within the sanctioners' utility functions, which are treated as assumptions, not variables. In addition, few scholars have examined racial equality in international politics; one notable exception is Paul Gordon Lauren, *Power and Prejudice: The Politics and Diplomacy of Racial Discrimination* (Boulder, Colo: Westview Press, 1988).

norms matter for sanctions in particular and international relations more broadly.

Reflecting the realist tradition in international relations theory, sanctions analysts tend to assume that multilateral sanctions are extremely difficult to implement because of conflicting national interests, and that coordinated implementation is essential.[5] Conventional theories generally claim that global issues and multilateral policies reflect the underlying military or economic distribution of capabilities. That South Africa, therefore, has been an important middle power and Western ally is unsurprising from conventional perspectives. But to explain the emergence of the apartheid issue and the adoption of sanctions, these theories would require evidence of structural military or economic change. Historical evidence does not support such a claim; the interests of great powers did not substantially change. For example, the pattern of steadily increasing international opposition to South Africa does not correspond to variations in East-West relations, and the United States adopted sanctions at the height of tensions with the Soviet Union.[6] Thus from a structural strategic perspective, apartheid—a domestic system of institutionalized racial discrimination—should never have gained global salience. In addition, traditional state-level (rather than systemic) realist perspectives might explain great power policies as resulting from the confluence of diverse strategic, economic, and ideological considerations, but they cannot explain either system-level convergence on sanctions or the fact that great powers followed, rather than initiated, demands for collective action against apartheid.[7]

Furthermore, from a structural economic perspective, we would expect to find opposition to apartheid only when institutionalized racial discrimination inhibited capitalist accumulation, since apartheid was instituted (proponents of such perspectives argue) in response to the

---

5. The former assumption reflects the realist orientation of most sanctions analysts. The latter reflects both the collective security "all against one" perspective (enshrined in the League of Nations and United Nations) and the importance of market conditions for sanctioned goods. For critiques of conventional theoretical assumptions in the sanctions literature, see David A. Baldwin, *Economic Statecraft* (Princeton: Princeton University Press, 1985), and Martin, *Coercive Cooperation*.

6. See especially Study Commission on U.S. Policy toward Southern Africa, *South Africa: Time Running Out* (Berkeley: University of California Press, 1981), and contributions in *African Crisis Areas and U.S. Policy*, ed. Gerald Bender, James S. Coleman, and Richard L. Sklar (Berkeley: University of California Press, 1985).

7. Contrast, for example, Hans J. Morgenthau, *Politics among Nations: The Struggle for Power and Peace*, 5th ed. (New York: Knopf, 1973), and Kenneth N. Waltz, *Man, the State, and War: A Theoretical Analysis* (New York: Columbia University Press, 1959).

economic needs of capitalism.[8] Historical evidence contradicts this claim at both the systemic and the regional levels. At the systemic level, opposition to South Africa is surprising since the country's socio-economic profile (including racial stratification) is similar to that of other industrializing countries, notably Brazil, that have never been subject to international sanctions; indeed, Western states supported capital infusions into South Africa after periods of economic and political upheaval in the 1960s and 1970s.[9] At the regional level, many southern African states challenged South African apartheid despite their structural economic dependence; transnational business interests supported reform efforts in South Africa only after apartheid became an international issue, and then only under anti-apartheid pressure.[10] Thus there is no theoretical or historical reason for us to expect actors (either countries or corporations) with economic interests to support costly international actions to promote changes in domestic South African legislation.

These conventional theoretical perspectives then fail to explain two crucial aspects of international reactions to apartheid: why racial discrimination within South Africa emerged as a global issue in a system based on sovereignty and domestic jurisdiction, and why most organizations and states adopted sanctions despite the strategic and economic interests that had previously ensured strong ties with South Africa. Because these perspectives stress the primacy of structural material interests, they cannot explain multilateral and bilateral policies adopted to support a norm of racial equality.

Little is understood of the causal mechanisms through which a norm such as racial equality produces multilateral and bilateral policies. In chapter 2, therefore, I explore the theoretical debates over international norms in order to extract analytical and methodological lessons

8. For a comparison of liberal and structural perspectives on apartheid, see Stanley B. Greenberg, "Economic Growth and Political Change: The South Africa Case," *Journal of Modern African Studies* 19 (December 1981), 667–704. In analyzing South African reform in the mid-1980s, Greenberg also argues that the government turned to market mechanisms to perpetuate discrimination when its coercive enforcement of apartheid laws proved decreasingly effective; see his *Legitimating the Illegitimate: State, Markets, and Resistance in South Africa* (Berkeley: University of California Press, 1987).

9. See William Minter, *King Solomon's Mines Revisited: Western Interests and the Burdened History of Southern Africa* (New York: Basic Books, 1986).

10. On regional economic dependency, see Ronald T. Libby, *The Politics of Economic Power in Southern Africa* (Princeton: Princeton University Press, 1987), and Joseph Hanlon, *Beggar Your Neighbors: Apartheid Power in Southern Africa* (Bloomington: Indiana University Press, 1986).

8

about policy to guide the subsequent empirical analysis. In contrast to the conventional theories that best explain continuities in South Africa's ties with Western great powers, I argue that a norm of racial equality plays crucial roles in defining identity and interest, rather than simply functioning as a weak constraint on more fundamental strategic or economic interests. Anti-apartheid sanctions, in other words, empirically illustrate more abstract interpretive theoretical claims concerning both the "constitutive" definition of group identities and interests (as nonracist) and the "regulative" definition of legitimate behavior and policy (as that which rejects racist discrimination).[11]

Multilateral policies toward South Africa demonstrate that neither realist political assumptions nor market economic conditions can explain the adoption (or rejection) of sanctions. Variations in sanctions policies across multilateral institutions show the importance of both collective interests and procedural rules. Multilateral policy does not simply reflect great powers' interests and goals. Rather, institutions can empower weak and nonstate actors, by setting agendas and defining group identities. The constitutive norms and decision-making procedures of these multilateral organizations explain the varying success of anti-apartheid activists in generating sanctions.

As chapter 3 demonstrates, South Africa's international isolation began in the United Nations through the efforts of Third World states and nongovernmental actors. As a norm of racial equality became increasingly codified in the UN General Assembly, Africans and their allies generated substantial opposition to apartheid. Following universally supported declarations condemning racial discrimination, apartheid opponents excluded South Africa from participation in most functional branches of the United Nations system and established new institutions to support the exiled South African anti-apartheid move-

11. I adopt the distinction between constitutive and regulative roles from Friedrich V. Kratochwil, *Norms, Rules, and Decisions: On the Conditions of Practical and Legal Reasoning in International Relations and Domestic Affairs* (Cambridge: Cambridge University Press, 1989). As I explain in chapter 2, this constitutive categorization takes norms beyond the intervening variable role as identified in both the standard definition of an international regime (as principles, norms, rules, and procedures that regulate particular issue areas) and recent work on the role of ideas as institutionalized road maps and focal points in foreign policy making. See, respectively, Stephen D. Krasner, "Structural Causes and Regime Consequences: Regimes as Intervening Variables," in his edited *International Regimes* (Ithaca: Cornell University Press, 1983), pp. 1–22, and Judith Goldstein and Robert O. Keohane, "Ideas and Foreign Policy: An Analytical Framework," in their edited *Ideas and Foreign Policy: Beliefs, Institutions, and Policy Change* (Ithaca: Cornell University Press, 1993), pp. 3–30.

ment. Anti-apartheid activists, however, were substantially less successful in garnering mandatory economic sanctions in the Security Council
owing to U.S. and British vetoes. Thus the anti-apartheid movement's
experience mitigates but does not completely refute realist skepticism
about international institutions. Anti-apartheid activists succeeded in
delegitimizing the South African government and legitimizing its opponents primarily where majority voting determined collective decisions.

Explaining anti-apartheid experiences in the Commonwealth according to conventional views of sanctions, however, remains more problematic. As I argue in chapter 4, African states and their allies forced
South Africa's withdrawal from the Commonwealth in 1961 despite
British dominance in the organization. Furthermore, advocates of racial equality won consensus on sanctions in the mid-1980s as part of
their broader efforts to redefine the organization as a multiracial,
rather than white colonial, institution. Leadership shifted to Australia,
Canada, India, and southern African states, leaving Britain to respond
to collective policy. The Commonwealth transformed itself, in the process, into a truly multilateral, rather than hegemonic, international institution.

In addition to losing its membership in the Commonwealth and
most branches of the United Nations, South Africa was excluded from
the Organization of African Unity from the institution's founding in
1963. As I explore in detail in chapter 5, the organization offered an
arena for defining African international and regional interests. After
determining collective policy, Africans actively advocated racial equality
and sanctions against South Africa in other international organizations,
such as the United Nations and the Commonwealth. In addition, African states provided crucial financial and logistical support to liberation
movements in southern Africa, sustaining substantial military, economic, and social costs for their advocacy of majority rule in the region. Conventional perspectives, however, overlook the importance of
collective African interest in eliminating racial discrimination.

Sanctions analysts also often assume that individual states will circumvent sanctions in pursuit of economic gain, causing inevitable gaps
in enforcement. While adopting rationalist assumptions about the primacy of cost-benefit calculations, conventional theorists emphasize material rather than social gains and losses. Affirming racial equality, however, can offer social benefits (such as enhancing collective identity and
promoting collective interests). The adoption of bilateral policies toward South Africa demonstrates that a narrow theoretical focus on eco-

nomic gains and losses fails to capture the social ways that states defined their interests and calculated costs. In particular, apartheid's emergence as a national issue in a range of states highlights variations in domestic race politics and their implications for foreign policy making.

Rather than initiating multilateral policies, as conventional perspectives would predict, the United States responded to transnational pressures at the same time that it rejected multilateral UN sanctions. As I explain in chapter 6, interest groups and activists connected to the transnational anti-apartheid movement linked domestic issues of civil rights and race relations to segregation in South Africa. In response to widespread domestic demands for sanctions, Congress passed legislation and overrode the veto of a popular president. Policy makers accepted the importance of promoting racial equality in South Africa despite immediate economic costs and strategic uncertainties, reversing long-standing assumptions that strategic and economic interests outweighed any benefits from promoting majority rule.

[margin note: racial equality outweighed econ. costs.]

As chapter 7 shows, transnational anti-apartheid activists in Britain proved less successful, although multilateral pressures nonetheless led the Thatcher government to modify its policy toward South Africa. A network of anti-apartheid activists similar to that in the United States had substantially less effect on policy because they lacked access to policy making in the British parliamentary system. In addition, the domestic discourse of race politics did not offer the salient connections that activists in the United States stressed. Yet international pressures within both the Commonwealth and the European Community garnered concessions from the British government. Despite its strong economic and military ties to South Africa, Britain adapted to multilateral demands for sanctions because of the social costs of appearing to tolerate racism.

[margin note: social costs of racial tolerance.]

While transnational and multilateral pressures altered great power policies, the question remains why advocates of racial equality—especially strategically and economically vulnerable southern African states—risked substantial material costs. To explain African opposition to South Africa, I examine Zimbabwean foreign policy in chapter 8. Zimbabwe's advocacy of sanctions and opposition to apartheid were rooted in the government's attempt to implement racial equality domestically, after gaining power from the white minority Rhodesians in 1980. Opposition to South Africa's apartheid policies became a touchstone for redefining domestic and regional interests. While Zimbabwe's own social transformation remained contested, as was evident in debates over collective African and national economic interests, the new majority rule government altered its regional policies to include military support for neighboring Mozambique. Zimbabwe suffered substantial economic and military costs for its domestic and international advocacy of racial equality, contrary to the predictions of conventional theories that discount the social side of states' interests.

Finally, most sanctions analysts argue that inflicting economic hardship on a target state may change its behavior, equating power with coercion.[12] South Africa's response to sanctions, however, offers evidence of the effects of both incentive and legitimation processes. Chapter 9 offers a preliminary analysis of the role of international sanctions in domestic South African reform and explores the implications for perspectives on power in the sanctions literature. Chapter 10 elaborates the broader theoretical implications of the role of norms and sanctions in legitimation processes. International and domestic debates over apartheid—and South Africa's future—cannot be understood unless we appreciate the power of race in defining identities and interests.

12. Baldwin, *Economic Statecraft*, chap. 2.

CHAPTER TWO

Norms in International Relations Theory

In international relations, because of the prevailing realist perspective, debates over the role of norms are often reduced to basic arguments about material interests versus ethical ideals. Realists characteristically reject norms as rationalizations for self-interest and deny them explanatory power. But if norms are solely a moral alternative to interests, only in the absence of motivations of interest would realists give credence to a norms explanation. All behavior, even altruism, can be reduced to individual rewards and interest explanations.[1] For example, we may give gifts in order to establish a relationship of reciprocity. Or perhaps gift giving makes us feel better about ourselves. Only pure altruism would motivate us to give gifts simply to benefit the recipient, although even in this scenario we might expect to enjoy the benefits of collective welfare in turn. In practice, actions are motivated by a complex combination of self-interest (the reciprocity relationship ensures our receiving gifts in the future), self-affirmation (we like to feel good about ourselves), and group interest (we like to make our friends happy).

To understand the role of norms, therefore, we should move beyond the paradigmatic division between the realists and the idealists. Conse-

---

1. Using various definitions, rationalists have modeled altruism through cost-benefit analyses. For an evaluation of these approaches, see Arthur A. Stein, *Why Nations Cooperate: Circumstance and Choice in International Relations* (Ithaca: Cornell University Press, 1990), pp. 164, 170–71. Particularly noteworthy is Amartya K. Sen's attempt to model ethical commitment in terms of metarankings of preference rankings; see his "Rational Fools: A Critique of the Behavioral Foundations of Economic Theory," in *Beyond Self-Interest*, ed. Jane J. Mansbridge (Chicago: University of Chicago Press, 1990), pp. 25–43.

quently, in this book I seek to gauge *how much* these components of self affirmation and group interest affect behavior and policy choices, by using material self-interest as a baseline. In the sanctions case, for example, explanations stressing structural material interests (such as realism and marxism) offer compelling reasons for many states' ties with South Africa. But since the material interest motivations for these policies remained generally constant, the shift to sanctions shows the expression of support for a norm of racial equality to be a plausible explanation for policy change.

I am defining norms broadly here, as shared (thus social) understandings of standards for behavior. Discrimination based on racially defined categories, evident in racist language, personal actions, or social policies, is bad, and individual equality (lack of racial discrimination) is good. Apartheid is then rejected as bad, as is support or tolerance for that system. By describing racism in such simplified terms, I do not intend to imply that all norms present clear and dichotomous alternatives. Nor are all norms moral, since these standards can have functional and nonethical origins and purposes. We will return to issues of defining and categorizing norms below.

The conditions under which self-affirmation and group interest affect policy, however, remain unclear. Why did some states and organizations adopt sanctions against South Africa decades before others? Institutional context—international regimes—offers one possible explanation. Combining regulative and procedural norms, regimes change the environment in which actors pursue their interests.[2] However, since actors' definitions of their interests remain constant in the standard formulation, these regime theorists accept the realist conception of norms as separate from, rather than constitutive of, interests.[3]

2. By characterizing regimes as regulative and procedural norms, I am translating the standard definition of regimes as principles, norms, rules, and procedures into two types of norms; compare Stephen D. Krasner, "Structural Causes and Regime Consequences: Regimes as Intervening Variables," in his edited *International Regimes* (Ithaca: Cornell University Press, 1983), p. 2.

3. There are important differences among regimes theorists. The neorealist, or modified realist, institutionalists stress the fundamental role of material interests and relative power among states in creating and changing institutional arrangements; see especially Stephen D. Krasner, *Structural Conflict: The Third World against Global Liberalism* (Berkeley: University of California Press, 1985), and Joseph M. Grieco, *Cooperation among Nations: Europe, America, and Non-tariff Barriers to Trade* (Ithaca: Cornell University Press, 1990). The neoliberal institutionalist perspective stresses the external costs and benefits to states in particular institutional arrangements; see especially Robert O. Keohane, *After Hegemony: Cooperation and Discord in the World Political Economy* (Princeton: Princeton Univer-

Consequently, conventional regimes theory offers little insight into self-affirmation and group-interest motivations, the identity dimensions of norms.

The regime critique of realism has nonetheless created a disciplinary opening for alternative institutionalist theories that do examine the constitutive role of norms through identity. Interpretivists, drawing broadly on literatures in social theory, philosophy, law, and literary criticism, advocate a more radical departure from the view that norms are the products of interests. In their critique of conventional structural theories, interpretive theorists argue that neorealism and neoliberalism are fundamentally incapable of capturing the importance of norms, for two reasons. First, norms are a fundamental component of both the international system and actors' definitions of their interests. Second, positivist epistemological and methodological assumptions are inherently incapable of capturing the crucial intersubjective aspect of norms. I use the interpretivist label to cover the broadest range of works that share these two theoretical claims.[4]

Applying this two-dimensional critique to an empirical analysis of sanctions policies—bridging the gap between abstract critiques of regime theories and positivists' demands for behavioral analysis—involves developing more specific explanatory claims about norms, interests, and identities. In the first section of this chapter I explore the implications of the interpretivist claim that norms should be analyzed as independent, and not solely intervening or dependent, variables at the system level. Then, responding to the epistemological and meth-

---

sity, 1984), and *International Institutions and State Power: Essays in International Relations Theory* (Boulder, Colo.: Westview Press, 1989). For a further contrasting of the neorealist and neoliberal institutionalists, see Grieco, *Cooperation among Nations*, and Keohane "Neoliberal Institutionalism: A Perspective on World Politics," in *International Institutions*, pp. 2, 14–16 (esp. nn. 1, 20). Despite Grieco and Keohane's disagreement over whether states are relative or absolute gain calculators, both are rationalist and structuralist because they share the basic assumption that states maximize their exogenously derived (material) interests; they disagree merely over the conditions in which states will calculate relative or absolute utilities.

4. Three variants of these interpretivist arguments are found in Friedrich Kratochwil and John Gerard Ruggie, "International Organization: A State of the Art on an Art of the State," *International Organization* 40 (Autumn 1986), 753–75; Richard K. Ashley, "The Poverty of Neo-Realism," in *Neorealism and Its Critics*, ed. Robert O. Keohane (New York: Columbia University Press, 1986), pp. 255–300; and Alexander Wendt, "Anarchy Is What States Make of It: The Social Construction of Power Politics," *International Organization* 46 (Spring 1992), 391–425. There are also significant differences among these scholars. Many postmodernists, in particular, would object to my emphasis on developing explanatory claims.

odological dimension of the interpretivist critique, that is, its claim that shared understandings are notoriously difficult to incorporate into theories of (international) politics, in the second section I explore conceptual clarifications, methodological tools, and carefully selected comparisons that enable us to overcome some of these difficulties.

SYSTEMIC NORMS AND INTEREST FORMATION

Interpretivists argue that we should consider states and the modern state system as constituted by a norm of sovereignty that emerged through political struggles in medieval Europe.[5] In the current international system, states exist because of a socially derived norm of sovereignty; this norm established territorial integrity and domestic (secular) political autonomy as essential to survival.[6] In some issue areas, especially war, sovereignty is usually acknowledged as the prevailing norm, but in others competing norms and nonstate actors play a larger role: in trade issues, for example, various norms that underpin the capitalist market system, such as private property rights. Property rights establish a variety of nonstate actors (such as firms or classes) and their interests (such as attaining capital or maximizing income) that lack the

[handwritten margin note: Private property establishes nonstate actors firms - classes]

5. John Gerard Ruggie argues that authority and territory were not coterminous and that they thus lacked the internal-external distinction that characterizes the modern concept of sovereignty. In addition, the medieval period was characterized by a diversity of actors and overlapping authorities. The emergence of notions of sovereignty and private property, furthermore, laid the basis for interstate relations and capitalism. See his "Continuity and Transformation in the World Polity: Toward a Neorealist Synthesis," in Keohane, *Neorealism and Its Critics*, pp. 131–57, as well as Friedrich Kratochwil, "Of Systems, Boundaries, and Territoriality: An Inquiry into the Formation of the State System," *World Politics* 39 (October 1986), 27–52. While emphasizing that sovereign states are socially constructed, Alexander Wendt places less emphasis on historical evolution; see his "Anarchy."

6. The particular processes by which sovereignty establishes authority and territorial integrity remain debated. Compare Janice E. Thomson, *Mercenaries, Pirates, and Sovereigns: State-Building and Extraterritorial Violence in Early Modern Europe* (Princeton: Princeton University Press, 1994); Stephen D. Krasner, "Westphalia and All That," in *Ideas and Foreign Policy: Beliefs, Institutions, and Political Change*, ed. Judith Goldstein and Robert O. Keohane (Ithaca: Cornell University Press, 1993), pp. 235–64; Robert H. Jackson, *Quasi-States: Sovereignty, International Relations, and the Third World* (Cambridge: Cambridge University Press, 1990); R. B. J. Walker, *Inside/Outside: International Relations as Political Theory* (Cambridge: Cambridge University Press, 1993); and Cynthia Weber, "Reconsidering Statehood: Examining the Sovereignty/Intervention Boundary," *Review of International Studies* 18 (1992), 199–216.

territorial boundaries of states.[7] More specifically, the transnational anti-apartheid movement existed because of its members' shared advocacy of a norm of racial equality. In addition, with human rights and democratization emerging more clearly as global issues, domestic jurisdiction is increasingly losing its salience. Consequently, across a wide range of issues, we no longer define survival—fundamental interests— solely in terms of territorial integrity and domestic political autonomy.

Thus interpretivists argue that international actors are inherently socially constructed; their identities and interests are partially defined by prevailing constitutive norms, which vary over time. Even if we accept states and anarchy as useful analytical tools for explaining war in the modern era, we must recognize that states and anarchy have not always existed. As a result, we must broaden our concept of system—and our understanding of changes across systems and within systems.[8] The distribution of military capabilities is no longer the sole and sufficient defining characteristic of an international system, and war between great powers is no longer the unique cause of system change. Constitutive norms are a crucial component of the international system.

Defining the system to include constitutive norms is an important conceptual shift, yet it creates neither an insurmountable disciplinary divide nor a rival paradigm.[9] If we replace the premise of states' essential autonomy with the broader interpretive assumption that constitutive norms can exist at the level of systems, we allow for an explanation

7. Alexander E. Wendt, "The Agent-Structure Problem in International Relations Theory," *International Organization* 41 (Summer 1987), esp. 345–47. Hedley Bull even considered property one of the three universal values of (international) society; see his *Anarchical Society: A Study of Order in World Politics* (New York: Columbia University Press, 1977), p. 5. On private property as a norm underpinning the market system, see Karl Polanyi, *The Great Transformation: The Political and Economic Origins of Our Time* (Boston: Beacon Press, 1957).

8. John Gerard Ruggie, "Territoriality and Beyond: Problematizing Modernity in International Relations," *International Organization* 47 (Winter 1993), 139–74; Walker, *Inside/Outside*.

9. Both practitioners and critics of the interpretive approach to international relations have characterized its emphasis on intersubjective meaning as the basis for an alternative to the conventional neorealist paradigm. From a neopositivist perspective, Robert O. Keohane has been prominent in creating this paradigmatic dichotomy through his distinction between "rationalists" and "reflectivists"; see his "International Institutions: Two Approaches," in *International Institutions and State Power*, pp. 158–79. Postmodernists also accept a dichotomy but from the perspective of "marginal voices"; see "Speaking the Language of Exile: Dissidence in International Studies," ed. Richard K. Ashley and R. B. J. Walker, special issue of *International Studies Quarterly* 34 (September 1990).

of the conditions under which states are relatively autonomous actors in a particular historical era. Interpretivists are currently exploring the empirical foundations for this argument, primarily in the transition between the medieval and modern periods, and previous historical studies by the British "international society" school further support the uniqueness of the modern period.[10]

Even if we are interested specifically in explaining changes within the current international system, this attention to the often implicit assumptions characteristic of historical eras is nonetheless important. Our analysis of racial equality, for example, assumes the context in which this particular norm has developed, that is, the Western liberal philosophical tenet of individual equality.[11] A norm of racial equality appears to have initially emerged through debates over slavery, which were framed by broader debates about the legitimacy of servitude versus wage labor within the emerging capitalist economic system. It strengthened with the emergence of a majority of nonwhite independent states following decolonization in the second half of the twentieth century.

The question arises, then, of how these systemic norms affect state interests. Interest formation is a crucial but unsolved issue for international relations theories.[12] All but the most avid neorealists agree that state interests are determined not simply by the structure of an anarchical interstate system defined in terms of military capabilities. Yet institutionalists disagree about the additional or alternative sources of those interests. Since regime theorists presume state autonomy but recognize limitations in structurally derived material-interest explanations, they search for a supplementary theory of interest formation through domestic politics, the only available direction given conventional levels of analysis.[13] One of the reasons such a theory remains elusive is that "do-

10. See especially Christian Reus-Smit, "The Moral Purpose of the State: Social Identity, Legitimate Action, and the Construction of International Institutions" (Ph.D. diss., Cornell University, 1995), and *The Expansion of International Society*, ed. Hedley Bull and Adam Watson (Oxford: Clarendon Press, 1984).

11. See esp. David Brion Davis, *Slavery and Human Progress* (New York: Oxford University Press, 1984), Robin Blackburn, *The Overthrow of Colonial Slavery 1776–1848* (London: Verso, 1988), and R. J. Vincent, "Racial Equality," in Bull and Watson, *Expansion of International Society*, pp. 239–54.

12. Keohane, "International Institutions"; Wendt, "Anarchy"; Stephan Haggard, "Structuralism and Its Critics: Recent Progress in International Relations Theory," in *Progress in Postwar International Relations*, ed. Emanuel Adler and Beverly Crawford (New York: Columbia University Press, 1991), pp. 403–37.

13. See Keohane, "International Institutions"; Andrew Moravcsik, "Introduction: Inte-

mestic factors" is a residual theoretical category that includes everything that cannot be explained through interstate structures or interaction.

In contrast, interpretivists posit that autonomous systemic norms, such as property rights or racial equality, may compete with sovereignty in a particular issue area. Consequently, interpretivists look to the shifting strength of these contending norms as a system-level explanation of interest formation. Social institutions (norms) are the product of actor interactions, while these actors' identities and interests in turn are defined by such social institutions.[14] Explaining the adoption of multilateral and bilateral sanctions policies toward South Africa, for example, involves analyzing the relationship between norms and sanctioners' goals, and not solely the role of international institutions in coordinating policy.

Figure 1 illustrates these conceptual differences between neorealism, regime theory, and interpretivist theory. As becomes clear from this illustration, regime theory is a subset of interpretive theory. Both approaches agree that international institutions matter in states' pursuit of their interests. The source of those interests becomes a broader research question, rather than an assumption. Interpretive theory does more than simply refute the regimes approach to norms; it asks under which conditions regime theories might offer us useful auxiliary, not core, explanations.

For example, a game-theoretical approach, popular in regime analysis, cannot be used to examine the interpretivist constitutive claim directly because structural constraints such as players, rules of the game, and payoffs are assumed. If the norms that underpin the international system are part of the explanation of the identity of players (including nonstate actors), the rules of interaction (including communicative language), and the nature of the payoff distribution (including actors'

---

grating International and Domestic Theories of International Bargaining," in *Double-Edged Diplomacy: International Bargaining and Domestic Politics,* ed. Peter B. Evans, Harold K. Jacobson, and Robert D. Putnam (Berkeley: University of California Press, 1993), pp. 3–42; Helen Milner, "International Theories of Cooperation among Nations: Strengths and Weaknesses," *World Politics* 44 (April 1992), 466–96.

14. Nicholas Greenwood Onuf, *World of Our Making: Rules and Rule in Social Theory and International Relations* (Columbia: University of South Carolina Press, 1989), and Wendt, "Anarchy," label this a "constructivist" approach based on Anthony Giddens's structuration theory, whose main tenet is that structures and agents reconstruct each other in a dynamic process of iteration. On Giddens, see David Held and John B. Thompson, eds., *Social Theory of Modern Societies: Anthony Giddens and His Critics* (Cambridge: Cambridge University Press, 1989).

Figure 1. Theories of norms and interests

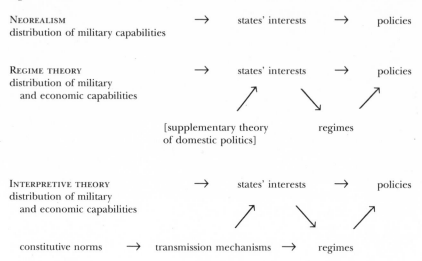

NEOREALISM   →   states' interests   →   policies
distribution of military capabilities

REGIME THEORY   →   states' interests   →   policies
distribution of military
  and economic capabilities

[supplementary theory   regimes
of domestic politics]

INTERPRETIVE THEORY   →   states' interests   →   policies
distribution of military
  and economic capabilities

constitutive norms   →   transmission mechanisms   →   regimes

interests or preferences), then interpretivist arguments can be used to explain the conditions that make certain game-theoretical models useful or inappropriate. Once we determine who the important players are and what they want, we can evaluate the likelihood that they will achieve their goals given the prevailing constraints.[15]

Viewing constitutive norms as autonomous—as opposed to dependent or intervening—thus shows interpretive theory as offering a set of prior, rather than alternative, theoretical assumptions. The result is a reformulated, complementary research agenda that illuminates the independent role of norms in determining actors' identities and interests. Combined with theories of institutions and interest-based behavior, this approach offers us a conceptually consistent and more complete understanding of international relations. But these claims, based on concepts such as identity, remain general. We still need to specify the mechanisms by which norms define and redefine identities and interests.

15. Thus Lisa L. Martin tests the difference between neorealism and neoliberalism but not interpretive or constructivist theory, because she assumes sanctioners' goals and interests; see her *Coercive Cooperation: Explaining Multilateral Economic Sanctions* (Princeton: Princeton University Press, 1992).

EXPLANATORY CLAIMS

Evaluating the explanatory power of interpretive theory first involves more precisely identifying competing theoretical claims about norms in four interrelated areas: (1) the origin of norms; (2) the causes of norm change; (3) the role of norms as constraints; and (4) the role of norms as motives. Particularly in the areas of constraint and motivation, significant conceptual differences emerge between interpretive and regime theories. Table 2 summarizes the contrasting theoretical claims in these four areas.

Table 2. Contending theoretical claims about norms

Conceptual issue	Regime theories	Interpretive theory
Origin of norms	Norms are imposed by a hegemon or generated *de novo* through actor (great power) interaction.	Norms are embedded in webs of existing (meta-) norms.
Cause of change	Norms change in accord with great power interests and capabilities.	Norms change through the influence of various state and nonstate actors.
Constraining role	Norms affect states' cost-benefit calculations.	Norms define social costs and benefits, especially through reputation.
Motivational role	Not directly applicable: interests are assumed.	Norms define interests and identities.

The Origin of Norms

Regime theorists offer two explanations for the origin of norms: hegemony and interaction.[16] Following their emphasis on material interests and coercion, neorealist institutionalists argue that norms reflect a hegemon's national interests or domestic values, revealing the origins of regime theory in debates over declining hegemony and the persis-

16. These correspond loosely to what Oran Young has labeled "negotiated" and "imposed" regimes; see his *International Cooperation: Building Regimes for Natural Resources and the Environment* (Ithaca: Cornell University Press, 1989), chap. 4. Although Young distinguishes further between "spontaneous" and "negotiated" regime formation, the interaction explanation shares characteristics of both, and Young himself acknowledges overlap of his "negotiated" and "imposed" categories (p. 88).

tence of international institutional arrangements.[17] Alternatively, focusing more on external incentives than coercion, neoliberals argue that norms are generated by actor interactions, and they frequently apply bargaining analyses within the general rubric of "cooperation under anarchy."[18] The research agenda of regime theory is to investigate the rival claims of these hegemony and interaction explanations.[19] Applying these theories to racial equality, a hegemonic dominance perspective would lead us to expect the United States in particular to export a norm of racial equality, while an interaction perspective would have us predict the emergence of the norm through recent negotiations, particularly between great powers.[20]

In contrast, interpretivists argue that new norms emerge from within previously existing social institutions. For example, in this view economic regimes such as the General Agreement on Tariffs and Trade should be analyzed in the context of established norms, including private property ownership, that define global capitalism.[21] Furthermore, global security regimes, that is, norms regulating strategic interaction, should be understood within the broader context of a prevailing Euro-

17. For example, see Krasner, *Structural Conflict*, and his "Sovereignty, Regimes, and Human Rights," in *Regime Theory and International Relations*, ed. Volker Rittberger (Oxford: Clarendon Press, 1993), pp. 139–67; and Albert O. Hirschman, "How the Keynesian Revolution Was Exported from the United States, and Other Comments," in *The Political Power of Economic Ideas: Keynesianism across Nations*, ed. Peter A. Hall (Princeton: Princeton University Press, 1989), pp. 347–60.

18. See, for example, Robert Axelrod, *The Evolution of Cooperation* (New York: Basic Books, 1984); contributions in *Cooperation under Anarchy*, ed. Kenneth A. Oye (Princeton: Princeton University Press, 1986); and Keohane, *After Hegemony*. However, since threats and coercion can also be analyzed in terms of cost and benefit, these hegemony (coercion) and interaction (incentive) perspectives are not mutually exclusive; see Stein, *Why Nations Cooperate*.

19. See esp. Grieco, *Cooperation among Nations*, and Martin, *Coercive Cooperation*.

20. I find no regime studies of the emergence of racial equality. Paul Gordon Lauren, in *Power and Prejudice: The Politics and Diplomacy of Racial Discrimination* (Boulder, Colo.; Westview Press, 1988), argues that prejudice declined only after the great powers adopted racial equality, but this classic realist position verges on tautology if we identify dominant norms by the compliance of great powers. Alternatively, a number of studies argue that hegemonic or great powers exported racial *inequality*: see Paul B. Rich, *Race and Empire in British Politics* (Cambridge: Cambridge University Press, 1986), as well as Vincent, "Racial Equality."

21. Friedrich Kratochwil emphasizes the importance of money as a social convention for underpinning exchange relationships; see his "On the Notion of 'Interest' in International Relations," *International Organization* 36 (Winter 1992), 19. John Gerard Ruggie makes a similar but more limited argument in "International Regimes, Transactions, and Change: Embedded Liberalism in the Postwar Economic Order," in Krasner, *International Regimes*, pp. 195–231.

pean culture.[22] To apply this emphasis on social context to questions of race, we can identify the origins of the norm of racial equality within liberal individualism.[23]

These disagreements over the origins of norms revolve around the question of the autonomy of norms, that is, the stability of norms and institutions despite changes in power distributions and actors' interests. Many regime theorists argue that while international norms may originally derive from great powers, they develop their own, limited autonomy by becoming institutionalized in international organizations and informal understandings. Interpretivists readily agree that norms become institutionalized but further add that norms need not be institutionalized in one organizational setting or in discrete issue areas. No "anti-apartheid regime" need exist for racial equality to be a significant norm. Nor are great powers necessarily the only agents of norm change; they may abide by norms rather than be their source. These theoretical differences also reveal themselves in similar debates over changes in norms.

The Causes of Norm Change

For both hegemonic and interaction regime theorists, changes in great powers' interests change the dominant norms (after a certain lag time). For those who see norms deriving from actor interactions, norm change can also be explained as the result of changing structural incentives such as costs and benefits. Regimes are stable if the international system is dominated by great powers or a hegemonic state that underwrites the short-term costs of regime maintenance, and institutions change in accord with broad alterations in the strength and interests of the dominant powers.[24] Applying the regime perspective to con-

22. On the conventions underlying the European security system, see Kratochwil, "On the Notion of 'Interest'"; Ruggie, "Continuity and Transformation"; Wendt, "Anarchy"; and Robert Jervis, "Security Regimes," in Krasner, *International Regimes*, pp. 173–94. For a non-European study of the security regime concept, see Neta C. Crawford, "A Security Regime among Democracies: Cooperation among Iroquois Nations," *International Organization* 48 (Summer 1994), 345–85. On the global expansion of European culture into a prevailing international culture, see contributions in Bull and Watson, *Expansion of International Society*.

23. For an analysis along these lines, see Vincent, "Racial Equality." Similar arguments are implicit, if not explicit, in studies of decolonization; see Robert H. Jackson, "The Weight of Ideas in Decolonization: Normative Change in International Relations," in Goldstein and Keohane, *Ideas and Foreign Policy*, pp. 111–38.

24. Thus Keohane and Grieco argue over whether states calculate their interests ac-

temporary questions of race, we would expect the norm of racial equality to strengthen only after a commitment from the United States.

While agreeing that the support of great powers may strengthen norms (and international institutions), interpretivists argue more broadly that norm change depends on the preexisting institutional structures in which actors are embedded. Norms may gain strength despite the interests of the great powers, or within broader institutions that were originally established with the support of great powers. Interpretivists might argue, for example, that colonial movements gained their independence—despite the opposition of many of the great powers—in the context of an institutionalized international norm of self-determination, which in turn was embedded within the broader context of state sovereignty.[25] Decolonization, in turn, produced a dramatic change in the distribution of power for the former colonial powers, with broad international military, economic, and ideological implications. Extending these arguments to race, the interpretivists emphasize that advocates of racial equality, such as these newly independent states, operated successfully within existing statecentric organizations despite great powers' opposition. Norms and institutions may empower weak and nonstate actors; anti-apartheid activists used international institutions to circumvent the opposition of the great powers.

Interpretivists and regime theorists agree that norms can at some point become reified, that is, can become regimes or social institutions that are part of the structure in which actors behave. Once a norm is only rarely contested, we can analyze its manifestation in institutions (ranging from organizations and treaties to informal understandings and shared expectations). In areas of research where norms are treated as intervening variables, methodological debates separate the contending approaches, but both refute the conventional materialist claim that norms are only epiphenomena.[26] The crucial question is then how a

---

cording to relative or absolute gains; structurally defined issue areas determine this different calculation. See especially Grieco, *Cooperation among Nations.* Krasner, in *Structural Conflict,* distinguishes between "metapower," which is the ability to set the rules of the game, and "relational power," which is the ability to achieve one's goals within the constraints of those rules. This view allows norms more autonomy from the states' interests, even though ultimately great powers determine norms.

25. Jackson, "Weight of Ideas." Interpretivists would thus not reject Krasner's notion of metapower but would disagree that only the powerful states determine these broader rules of the game, the "metanorms."

26. Oran Young's work exemplifies the compatibility of these research agendas; see his *International Cooperation* and "The Effectiveness of International Institutions: Hard

contested norm, such as racial equality, becomes institutionalized, both globally and domestically.

Constraints

Norms as Constraints

Evaluating autonomy—the causal importance—of norms usually involves debates over the external constraining power of norms: the degree to which (powerful) actors comply with an international norm. In its simplest form, realists remind us, international law lacks the autonomous power to constrain actors against the imperatives of their interests; only coercion explains a state's compliance with a norm. Prevailing norms, in the realist view, reflect the interests of the great powers because those are the only norms that are coercively enforced. Despite their willingness to acknowledge coercive power under certain conditions, however, institutionalists present different arguments in defending the importance of international norms.

Building on their assumptions about the origins of norms, regime theorists have two explanations for compliance with norms. The hegemonic perspective resembles the basic realist perspective but grants limited normative constraint, while the interaction perspective explains compliance primarily in terms of incentives. When reciprocity prevails, norms get institutionalized because such arrangements provide benefits (such as information in an uncertain world) that outweigh the opportunity costs of foregoing immediate action in their short-term interests. Under certain conditions, states willingly bear costs for maintaining regimes even in the absence of hegemonic coercion. International institutions, functioning like economic markets, induce cooperation by altering the incentives that actors face.[27]

Interpretivists articulate a broader legitimating role for norms, one that includes determining appropriate means as well as goals.[28] Military actions may be considered a legitimate option for defensive purposes in the current international system, yet other goals, such as territorial expansion, that were legitimate in earlier periods, no longer are. The Iraqi

---

Cases and Critical Variables," in *Governance without Government: Order and Change in World Politics,* ed. James Rosenau and Ernst-Otto Czempiel (Cambridge: Cambridge University Press, 1992), pp. 160–94.

27. Martin's empirical evaluation of these claims supports the importance of institutions; see *Coercive Cooperation,* esp. chap. 9.

28. See Friedrich Kratochwil, "The Force of Prescriptions," *International Organization* 38 (Autumn 1984), 685–708, and Ernst B. Haas, "Why Collaborate? Issue-Linkage and International Regimes," *World Politics* 32 (April 1980), pp. 357–405.

invasion of Kuwait in August 1990 provoked multilateral sanctions because UN members defined its action as aggressive territorial expansion. Protesting racial discrimination in South Africa might lead specifically to the adoption of sanctions because of this legitimation of means. Thus while regimes theorists analyze norms narrowly, in terms of their influence on the choice of a given set of legitimate means, interpretivists analyze the effect of prevailing norms on determining that set.

Norms as Motives

Even more profoundly than legitimizing means, however, norms legitimize goals and thus define actors' interests and their overarching world views. Most regime theorists acknowledge that their approach does not explain goals or interests, although, they argue, one role norms play is to institutionalize long-term interest calculations. Game-theoretical analyses, for example, emphasize "a shadow of the future" and iterative play to explain the development of reciprocity.[29] As illustrated in Figure 1, regime theory can treat interest formation only as exogenous domestic factors.

In contrast, by focusing on global processes of norm change, interpretivists can avoid isolating domestic political processes from international or transnational influences, as would occur with a sovereignty assumption and conventional levels of analysis.[30] Domestic strengthening of a norm of racial equality might thus result from broader transnational processes of norm strengthening. It is this claim that interests can be explained endogenously within the international system, through norms, that most clearly illustrates interpretivism's divergence from regime theory and offers grounds for empirical analysis.

Drawing on this overview of interpretive theory, we can construct two general hypotheses about the relationship between norms and interests: First, the emergence or strengthening of a global constitutive norm is likely to lead to changes in actors' interests and identities, potentially including the creation of new actors. Second, a change in interests, as well as the possible emergence of new actors, is likely to

29. See Stein, *Why Nations Cooperate*, chap. 4. Keohane's concept of "diffuse reciprocity" comes closest to capturing the interpretivist position; see "Reciprocity in International Relations," in *International Institutions and State Power*, chap. 6.

30. See, for example, Emanuel Adler and Peter M. Haas, "Conclusion: Epistemic Communities, World Order and the Creation of a Reflective Research Program," special issue on "Knowledge, Power, and International Policy Coordination," *International Organization* 46 (Winter 1992), 367–90.

produce regulative norms that will be compatible with the new or strengthened constitutive norm. We would then expect these regulative norms to influence policy choices through processes of coercion, inducement, and legitimation, as explained by the various institutionalist theories.

Two corresponding types of political processes characterize continuity and change in this norm-based international system: in constitutive terms, struggles to define the mutual understandings (assumptions such as state sovereignty, private property, and individual equality) that underpin identities, rights, grievances, and interests; and in instrumental terms, attempts to control behavior through a wide range of social sanctions, of which the use of military force is only one. Acknowledging and understanding these two distinct processes means going beyond narrow conceptions of power based on objective capabilities to consider how actors also maintain and propagate their visions of good and bad, justice and injustice, or conducive and nonconducive environments.

To the extent that these "symbolic" struggles over the ranking of norms affect the agendas and allocation of resources in international arenas and within states, they have significant "real world" consequences. By positing a constitutive relationship between norms and interests, interpretive theory moves us beyond the realist-idealist dichotomy and on to questions of how to analyze self-affirmation and group interest empirically.

EVALUATING NORMS

Having identified legitimation as a crucial component of both constraint and motivation, we can distinguish and analyze the constitutive, regulative, and procedural roles of norms beyond the simple, and insufficient, behavioral evidence of compliance. A few additional concepts and tools help us concentrate on the transmission mechanisms that link norms and policy choice. First, considering international "communities" (rather than a single international society) as sites of identity and interest formation allows us to observe variations in policy that are due to change in memberships and external norms. Second, by analyzing actors' "reputations," defined with reference to prevailing norms, we can observe the legitimation processes and their noncoercive constraining effects that interpretive theorists claim reinforce identities and create interests. Third, by examining international and domestic discourse, as well as more formal institutions, we can trace the impact of norms in policy-making processes. The remainder of this chapter explores these strategies for carrying out empirical analysis of norms and identities.

Community and Identity

Interpretivists argue that identity and interests depend on sociohistorical context. To reinforce this theoretical claim, we need to demonstrate empirically that identities and interests change in different contexts. Short of a macrohistorical analysis (whose aim is not to explain policy choice), this is a difficult task if we look at only a single international system (or society). Differentiating the international system into subsystemic communities helps us disaggregate the notion of a dominant international order. These communities develop out of shared values and interests based on multiple, rather than single-issue, relationships; any state may maintain several simultaneous community memberships or group identities.[31] For example, membership in the European Community involves adopting various identity-defining norms, such as maintaining a democratic form of government. In contrast, membership in the United Nations is based on a general norm of sovereign statehood. This anthropological notion of community is a useful heuristic for focusing on the constitutive norms that define collectivities of actors, and we can use foundational principles, as well as collective articulations of threat, as indicators of identity distinct from interests and behavior.[32]

31. I base this notion of communities on what anthropologist F. G. Bailey characterizes as "multiplex" rather than single-interest relationships. See his "Gifts and Poison" and "Changing Communities," in his edited *Gifts and Poison: The Politics of Reputation* (New York: Schocken, 1971), pp. 1–25, 26–40. In this book I do not try to establish criteria for defining the dichotomous existence or absence of community, particularly since such a relationship depends on participating actors' interpretations of a special relationship. States themselves thus form a community, based on shared interests and common identity of their citizens. Compare Walker, *Inside/Outside*.

32. To avoid an ex post facto argument, it is essential to trace the development of these communities historically prior to the emergence of the issue or policy decision being analyzed. This would involve, for example, empirically identifying states' articulation of identities, that is, whether they consider themselves "European," "African," "liberal," "civilized," "capitalist," "socialist," "democratic," and so on. These identities are not essential characteristics that can be determined by a list of "objective" criteria abstracted from the sociohistorical context. Discourse analysis is a particularly useful methodologi-

In addition, a nonuniversal concept of community circumvents structural determinism by adding an element of choice and acceptability to sets of norms and group identities; since membership within various communities is possible, we need not rely on functional logic. States may remain members of institutional arrangements for identity-affirming reasons, as well as for material gains. For example, while one could argue that the Commonwealth emerged out of the needs of a postcolonial British hegemony, its strength and importance increased with the decline in British power. Furthermore, given the range of possible communities, it is not surprising that a state should be simultaneously a member of groupings that are founded upon inconsistent, if not contradictory, norms.[33] Britain's European Community membership initially conflicted with its Commonwealth membership (particularly on economic issues), and both of these conflicted with its obligation of general reciprocity under the General Agreement on Tariffs and Trade. Membership choice helps us assess evolving consensus and conflict over dominant norms.

If interpretive theorists are right that actors affirm their identities and legitimize their actions within the framework of prevailing norms, then these communities are crucial arenas in which identities influence actor behavior. Membership offers social costs and benefits, not solely economic or functional incentives. Behavior takes on different meanings depending on the context and the legitimation proffered. Community standards define how far behavior can diverge from norms, enabling sanctions to work as instruments of socialization through identity constraint and identity affirmation.

Reputation and Communication

This focus on affirmation and legitimation—the intersection of language and practice—has prompted many interpretive theorists to argue for methodologies that identify norms not solely through behavioral outcomes but also through communicative processes. Focusing on communicative interactions shifts attention away from choices between structures or agents and toward the fundamentally shared or intersub-

---

cal strategy; see esp. David Campbell, *Writing Security: United States Foreign Policy and the Politics of Identity* (Minneapolis: University of Minnesota Press, 1992). Here I do not attempt to explain the origin of specific community identities.

33. See especially Michael Barnett, "Institutions, Roles, and Disorder: The Case of the Arab States System," *International Studies Quarterly* 37 (September 1993), 271–96.

jective nature of norms. By analyzing communication, we can identify norms nontautologically through both justifications and actions, avoiding the problems of falsifiability that arise since behavior contrary to norm prescription does not necessarily invalidate the norm. Thus "intentionality" and "acceptability," rather than mere behavioral compliance or deviance, become central to our understanding the constraining effects of international identity and norms.[34] Once we accept these processes of legitimation and socialization as theoretically important, we can analyze identity through reputation.

If tracing legitimation or socialization empirically involves understanding communicative interaction, we need to analyze actors' words and intentions separately from their behavior. A focus on the characteristic of reputation posits the type of relationship between language and behavior that theorists claim is essential.[35] Since reputation is defined by the opinions of others, it is a relational, not an essential, quality. Thus normative constraint depends on how a deviant is perceived by other community members, and specifically on how others have interpreted its actions. A community relationship defines which actors matter, that is, whose judgments matter, who the receivers of justifications are, and whose sanctions are of most concern to the deviant.[36]

Reputation therefore becomes a source of vulnerability and a potential constraint on an actor's ability to achieve its goals; however, the

34. Inferences from behavior frequently lead to tautologous definition of actors' interests, as does the risky method of revealed preferences. See Kratochwil and Ruggie, "International Organization," p. 766, and Duncan Snidal, "The Game *Theory* of International Politics," in Oye, *Cooperation under Anarchy*, pp. 25–57.

35. The conventional notion of reputation in game theory offers only limited parallels; it has a much narrower focus on an actor's reputation for trustworthiness and favors parsimonious explanations, leading to a concentration on dyadic (rather than more complex) relationships and the need for unambiguous categories such as discrete payoffs. Although actors may themselves interact, there remains a third party, the community, that is also judging and evaluating. For elaboration see William Goode, *Celebration of Heroes: Prestige as a Social Control System* (Berkeley: University of California Press, 1978). Parsimonious theory seeks to avoid complexity and ambiguity, which are essential characteristics of norms and the interpretations of shared norms.

36. Michael Taylor, in *Anarchy, Community, and Liberty* (Cambridge: Cambridge University Press, 1982), argues theoretically that it is precisely these processes of judgment, justification, and sanction at the community level that are crucial to the maintenance of social order in stateless societies. Studies in political anthropology confirm such socialization processes; for a broad overview, see James C. Scott, *Domination and the Arts of Resistance: Hidden Transcripts* (New Haven: Yale University Press, 1990), and his earlier case study, *Weapons of the Weak: Everyday Forms of Peasant Resistance* (New Haven: Yale University Press, 1985).

consequences of a negative reputation will vary in seriousness. Some degree of deviation from the community standards helps to define those norms, as with the early condemnation of apartheid in the United Nations. Responses to repeated deviation will depend in part on the types of norms being flouted and the previous reputation of the deviant. Recurring or extreme deviations can lead to serious consequences, including expulsion from the community. South Africa's withdrawal from the Commonwealth followed this pattern, as did its exclusion from the Organization of African Unity. Especially if accompanied by substantial sanctions against it, a country's development of a negative reputation can have serious ramifications, as evident in the experiences of pariah states. (Pariahs may also benefit from such exclusion, as the outcast is then also free of obligations to the community. South Africa, for example, avoided obligations to provide development funds and international monitoring of its nuclear energy program.) The norms by which behavior is judged, therefore, set the boundaries of political conflict and cooperation.

Although unable to determine their own reputations, actors can try to convey a particular image in order to minimize any negative repercussions of community criticisms. Attempting to be associated with and evaluated through the framework of the community's shared values by emphasizing desirable traits, they may show certain sides in different contexts and communities. Presumably, the more interactions an actor has with other community members, the more developed its reputation will be, while fewer interactions would permit more control of its image. As a result, an actor's community relations largely involve the control (or manipulation) of information in attempts to fit into the normative frameworks within which other members evaluate its actions. Their use in encouraging cooperation or compliance adds an instrumental role to norms and justifications.[37] For example, the Thatcher government endeavored repeatedly, and ultimately unsuccessfully, to establish credible sympathy for blacks within South Africa as a justification for rejecting anti-apartheid sanctions. Thus the ability to communicate becomes critical for navigating through the constraining effects of identity in the form of reputation.

37. F. G. Bailey, "The Management of Reputations and the Process of Change," in his *Gifts and Poison*, pp. 281–301. David D. Laitin characterizes this instrumental aspect as the second side of the "Janus face" of culture; see his exchange with Aaron Wildavsky, "Political Culture and Political Preferences," *American Political Science Review* 82 (June 1988), 589–91.

Discourse and Institutions

Discourse and institutions guide us to the motivational dimension of norms, linking identity and interests, on the one hand, and policy and behavior, on the other. Through international and domestic decision-making processes, various avenues exist for norms, as embodied in individuals' beliefs or embedded in social discourse, to influence the determination of national interests and political goals. Among these transmission mechanisms are multilateral institutional memberships, bilateral persuasion or learning, elite changes, domestic coalition building, and more dramatic domestic social transformation.[38] These international and domestic policy-making institutions may also remain insulated from new norms. Variation across decision-making institutions is thus one important area for empirical interpretive analysis.

Yet examining decision-making processes through individual motivation and cognition alone ignores the commonality of shared norms underlying dominant ideas or knowledge. While any individual holds a unique, subjective conception of "reality," through social interaction individual ideologies develop into shared, intersubjective, community conceptions of normality and deviance, which produce relatively consistent interpretations of the empirical world.[39] Norms, as guides for understandings, are crucial in defining and shaping reactions to the world they interpret. Consequently, these intersubjective understand-

---

38. For examples, see Joseph S. Nye, Jr., "Nuclear Learning and U.S.-Soviet Security Regimes," *International Organization* 41 (Summer 1987), 371–402; Emanuel Adler, *The Power of Ideology: The Quest for Technological Autonomy in Argentina and Brazil* (Berkeley: University of California Press, 1987); Judith Goldstein, "The Impact of Ideas on Trade Policy," *International Organization* 43 (Winter 1989), 31–72; Ernst B. Haas, *When Knowledge Is Power: Three Models of Change in International Organizations* (Berkeley: University of California Press, 1990); contributions in *The Political Power of Economic Ideas: Keynesianism across Nations,* ed. Peter A. Hall (Princeton: Princeton University Press, 1989); Kathryn Sikkink, *Ideas and Institutions: Developmentalism in Brazil and Argentina* (Ithaca: Cornell University Press, 1991); and contributions in "Knowledge, Power, and International Policy Coordination," ed. Peter M. Haas, special issue of *International Organization* 46 (Winter 1992).

39. One alternative to behavior-inferred identification of norms is a focus on the role of individual decision makers' beliefs and the effect of norms on personal perceptions. Proponents of this method argue for inductive analysis based upon personal interviews and written statements of rules to illuminate the decision-making process. Although convincing on the importance of avoiding tautologous proof of norms through behavioral evidence, these scholars presume that codification of rules is the crucial site of norms, that such rules do indeed affect behavior, and that interviewees will be able to illuminate their "true" decision-making process. Compare, e.g., Donald J. Puchala and Raymond F. Hopkins, "Lessons from Inductive Analysis," in Krasner, *International Regimes,* pp. 61–91.

ings—the standards by which behavior is judged—are also essential in setting the boundaries of political struggle or cooperation.

Thus rather than depending only on individuals' beliefs or understandings, policy-making processes involve shared assumptions about the political process and national interests. Focusing on consistencies in assumptions within decision-making processes—evident in discourse—reduces our dependence on divining individuals' thoughts and motivations, reasserts the importance of shared norms, and offers a tool for tracing changes in dominant global norms to the domestic decision-making processes. Examining discourse is a key area for applying process-tracing methodologies.

In the anti-apartheid case, we will observe variations in the permeability of decision-making institutions to a norm of racial equality, leading multilateral organizations and states to adopt different types of sanctions and complementary policies, including giving aid to South Africa's neighboring states and exiled anti-apartheid activists. South Africa's opponents made less progress in institutions where advocating a norm of racial equality conflicted with the prevailing discourse. For example, in the UN General Assembly, the call for racial equality in South Africa meshed with the prevailing emphasis on equality and anti-Nazism, but in the Security Council, permanent members rejected the argument that apartheid created a threat to international peace and security. Similarly, the U.S. Congress adopted sanctions once anti-apartheid activists successfully linked South African racial discrimination to domestic race relations, but the British government stayed immune to similar domestic demands for sanctions in part because of the lack of a domestic discourse of racial equality. Table 3 summarizes these conditions and cases. This hypothesis, that variations in the permeability of discourse and decision-making processes affect policy, deserves further studies. It may be plausible as a more general explanation of the conditions under which norms redefine interests.

Cases and Comparisons

As Table 3 illustrates, opponents of apartheid advocated the same norm across a variety of contexts. The differences between the cases highlight conflicts over racism and racial equality, clearly identifying a contested norm. In the chapters that follow, I establish the conditions under which apartheid did (or did not) become an issue in each multilateral organization and state. I then explore what responses these ac-

Table 3. International reactions to apartheid

	Discourse	Key actors	Decision making	Policy
MULTILATERAL				
UN General Assembly	Equality	African states, Third World allies	Majority vote	Voluntary sanctions, liberation support
UN Security Council	Threat to peace and security	Permanent members	Veto power	Mandatory arms embargo
Commonwealth	Multiracialism	African states, Britain, Canada, Australia, the secretary-general	Consensus	Voluntary sanctions, regional aid
Organization of African Unity	Liberation	Founders, Frontline states	Majority vote, consensus	Exclusion from membership, preemptive sanctions, liberation support
BILATERAL				
United States	National interests, race relations	Executive, Congress, interest groups	Separation of powers	Economic and military sanctions
Britain	National interests, race relations	Prime minister, party leaders	Cabinet decisions	Minor sanctions, regional aid
Zimbabwe	National interests, race relations	Prime minister, party leaders	Cabinet decisions	Partial sanctions, regional military action, liberation support

tors considered appropriate by identifying the range of legitimate policy options, including the reasons some rejected sanctions. Their justifications show the extent to which actors attempt to legitimize their policy choices and illustrate how advocates of racial equality clashed with proponents of apartheid, generating global debate over constitutive norms and material interests.

Since debates over apartheid took place in most international arenas and within most great powers, we can explore variations across communities and actors by asking when and why apartheid became an international issue in a system based on sovereignty and domestic jurisdiction, and when and why states adopted anti-apartheid sanctions despite strategic and economic interests. Thus the controversy surrounding South African apartheid offers numerous chances to compare processes of international legitimation, including the transmission of global norms into domestic foreign policy-making processes.

I examine three international organizations: the United Nations, the

Commonwealth, and the Organization of African Unity. These three arenas represent what were (and remain) the three sides of South Africa's international identity at the beginning of the postwar era: global-European, British-colonial, and African. In chapters 3, 4, and 5, I look at the context in which apartheid was debated, the key actors in those debates, the decision-making institutions in which the actors resolved their differences, and their resulting policy choices. I argue that variations across these arenas demonstrate the importance of different prevailing discourses and institutional decision-making procedures for the promotion of debates about apartheid and sanctions.

Similarly, to compare competing interest explanations for states' policies, I analyze the cases of three countries: the United States, Britain, and Zimbabwe. These cases, all countries with strong military and economic ties with South Africa, capture a range of variation in reactions to apartheid. The three states' foreign policies represent the bilateral dimension of South Africa's defining identities; the global-European, the British-colonial, and the African dimensions, respectively. Emphasizing the conceptual similarities in decision-making procedures between states and international organizations, in chapters 6, 7, and 8 I again address the context of the apartheid debates, the key actors, the relevant institutions, and their resulting policies. Again I conclude that differences among domestic discourses and decision-making processes are crucial.

While the success of anti-apartheid pressure in favor of sanctions policies illustrates the importance of race, and opposition to racism, as both a source of external pressure and an internal motivation for policy change, this interpretivist analysis reaffirms the usefulness of interest-based explanations. Interpretation can help us to understand the sources of interests, rather than merely to posit that norms contradict motivations based solely on interest. In other words, clarifying that interpretivists are explaining interests as well as policies is a crucial step in bridging the conceptual divide between rationalist and postmodern theorists of international relations.

PART II

MULTILATERAL POLICIES

CHAPTER THREE

The United Nations

Traditionally, debates over sanctions focus on the United Nations because article 2, chapter 7 of its charter empowers the Security Council to adopt mandatory and comprehensive measures. Analysts frequently conclude that sanctions are an inherently difficult, if not fundamentally flawed, policy since consensus among the permanent members of the Security Council is an elusive goal.[1] Both the United Nations as an institution and sanctions as a multilateral policy, in the realist view, remain mere instruments of hegemonic powers. To realists, issues of human rights reflect the interests and concerns of great powers, and hegemonic regime theorists in turn explain what conditions lead to the institutionalization of those concerns.[2] Although the United States and Britain did consistently block mandatory economic sanctions against South Africa, the Security Council nonetheless adopted a mandatory arms embargo. UN sanctions against South Africa thus require a more detailed analysis if we are to explain this apparent anomaly.

More optimistically, neoliberal institutionalists stress that the great powers may use the UN system to encourage cooperation for sanctions by adding incentives for coordinated multilateral policies.[3] While an institutionalist perspective predicts differences between the General As-

1. For an overview of skeptical views of sanctions, see David A. Baldwin, *Economic Statecraft* (Princeton: Princeton University Press, 1985).

2. For example, see Stephen D. Krasner, "Sovereignty, Regimes, and Human Rights," in *Regimes Theory and International Relations*, ed. Volker Rittberger (Oxford: Clarendon Press, 1993), pp. 139–67.

3. See especially Lisa L. Martin, *Coercive Cooperation: Explaining Multilateral Economic Sanctions* (Princeton: Princeton University Press, 1992).

sembly and Security Council, as indeed occurred with numerous voluntary sanctions that hinged on majority voting rather than permanent member veto, the neoliberal perspective persists in emphasizing the leadership of the great powers. In the South African case, however, a broad coalition of African and Asian members led the sanctions movement in the face of great power opposition. Since such agenda setting by weak states and nonstate actors (the nascent anti-apartheid movement) is an anomaly from conventional theoretical perspectives, it also deserves further attention.

The experience of anti-apartheid activists in the UN system as a whole mitigates realist skepticism about the role of institutions and the possibilities for multilateral sanctions policies, and partly supports the claims of regime theorists. Furthermore, the South African case demonstrates legitimation processes at work, as interpretivists argue.[4] In this chapter I first explore UN debates in the General Assembly and Security Council in order to explain why apartheid became an international issue in a system based on sovereignty. Then I examine the range of anti-apartheid policies that the United Nations adopted against South Africa. These policies demonstrate that actors supported a norm of racial equality, I argue, and that they adopted sanctions both to signal their support for the norm and to affect South Africa's domestic policy of racial segregation.

Racial Equality Supersedes Sovereignty

During the 1940s and 1950s, support for racial equality grew, and concern over apartheid emerged within the more general context of the postwar human rights agenda. The first decades of UN debate and activism generally established the universality of these rights and general standards for state practice.[5] But more clearly than in other cases involving human rights, the condemnation of apartheid generated ac-

4. John Gerard Ruggie, "Human Rights and the Future International Community," *Daedalus* 112 (Fall 1983), 93–110. Inis L. Claude, Jr. distinguishes between the principles used in legitimation and the process of legitimation in "Collective Legitimation as a Political Function of the United Nations," *International Organization* 20 (Summer 1966), 369–70.

5. David P. Forsythe, "The United Nations and Human Rights, 1945–1985," *Political Science Quarterly* 100 (Summer 1985), pp. 249–69; Gene M. Lyons, "In Search of Racial Equality: The Elimination of Racial Discrimination," in *Global Issues in the United Nations Framework*, ed. Paul Taylor and A. J. R. Groom (New York: St. Martin's, 1989), pp. 75–115.

tions as well as general, voluntary resolutions. Once advocates had established the universality of the norm of racial equality in the early 1960s, sanctions followed.

The Rise of Racial Equality

Before controversy over its racial policies emerged, South Africa had been an important international actor. For example, its prime minister, Jan Smuts, was influential in the design of the UN Charter as well as the earlier League of Nations Covenant. The country's international prestige started to tarnish as early as 1946, however, when its racial policies were debated at the United Nations' first session. Though unsuccessful in deflecting criticism of his domestic policies, Smuts retained his interest in international participation rather than reverting to isolationism. South Africa therefore remained a target of international criticism. (In contrast, the opposition National Party took a more isolationist view and frequently criticized Smuts for paying too much attention to international affairs and subjecting the country to international interference.)[6] Thus in the late 1940s, critics of South Africa's domestic and international affairs focused their efforts on the United Nations.

At the first session of the United Nations in 1946, India raised the issue of the treatment of Indian nationals in the Union of South Africa, a contentious issue in Indian–South African relations since 1907. Indians originally came to South Africa as indentured laborers, to be sent home after their term of service. South Africa at times allotted land in lieu of the agreed-upon free return ticket to India, although the government claimed never to have abandoned the principle of ultimate repatriation. Britain and India insisted, however, that South Africa grant these Indians citizenship rights. Efforts at repatriation in the late 1920s failed, and tensions increased. Subsequent legislation such as the Pegging Act restricted Indian settlement and land ownership.[7] In previous years the two governments had quarreled within the British

6. In particular, the opposition criticized Smuts for taking the issue of incorporation of South West Africa (Namibia) to the United Nations, rather than proceeding unilaterally. On Smuts's internationalism, see James Barber and John Barratt, *South Africa's Foreign Policy: The Search for Status and Security 1945–1988* (Cambridge: Cambridge University Press, 1990), pp. 15–20 and, for nationalist criticism of his approach to Namibia, p. 22. The National Party adopted a more isolationist policy after coming to power in 1948.

7. For an overview of segregation in the 1940s and early 1950s, see Leonard Thompson, *A History of South Africa* (New Haven: Yale University Press, 1990), pp. 178–200.

Empire (as India was not yet independent), but India brought the issue to the United Nations for what it considered to be South Africa's failure to honor previous agreements regarding rights. The formation of the United Nations presented India with a new opportunity to seek resolution of the issue.

UN members first considered whether the previous agreements between South Africa and India were treaties and appropriate subject matter for consideration. Debates revolved around interpretation of the new UN Charter. Not surprisingly, South Africa invoked the norm of noninterference in domestic affairs in its efforts to keep its policies off the international agenda. It argued that the people concerned were nationals (of Indian origin) of the Union of South Africa, rather than Indian nationals, and consequently, that the agreements between the two countries were not treaties and therefore were not internationally binding. In response to criticisms of human rights violations inconsistent with the UN Charter, South Africa cited the lack of any internationally recognized formulation of such rights, claiming that the charter did not involve specific obligations.

Against the United Nations' focus on individual rights, South Africa defended group rights. It argued that giving primacy to individual rights "was tantamount to saying that the most progressive races should be retarded by the less progressive if the latter were in the majority. Equality in fundamental rights and freedom could be assured in a multi-racial State only by a measure of discrimination in respect of non-fundamental rights."[8] Because of the priority it accorded to the survival of whites as a group, apartheid proponents claimed to champion group rights and presented South Africa's political difficulties as an unavoidable result of its multiethnic or multiracial composition. Since international consensus on fundamental human rights was still in its formative stage, South Africa sought to deflect criticism by rejecting the primacy of individual rights.

Although many other states supported South Africa's claim to domestic jurisdiction, the majority agreed to include the Indian issue on the agenda. Expecting to find agreement that no binding formulation of rights existed, the South African government pushed for an International Court of Justice advisory opinion on competency. After agreeing

8. Department of Information of the United Nations, *Yearbook of the United Nations* (New York: Columbia University Press/United Nations), 1946–47, p. 146. Ironically, the same year the National Party came to power proclaiming the philosophy of apartheid (1948), the United Nations agreed to the Universal Declaration of Human Rights.

to consider the issue jointly in both the political and security (first) and legal (sixth) committees of the General Assembly, many members opposed South Africa's proposal for this advisory opinion because they considered the political questions to outweigh the legal ones. These states also claimed that signing the charter involved both a degree of renunciation of domestic sovereignty and an obligation to refrain from policies based on racial discrimination.[9] The first resolution adopted, 44 (I), established that the treatment of the Indian population of South Africa was an issue of UN concern but merely requested further reports from the governments of the two countries involved.

In a tactical shift, in 1952 India put forth the first motion specifically concerning the practice of apartheid, hoping that abolishing racial discrimination would bring equal rights to both Asians and Africans.[10] Consideration of apartheid as a separate agenda item also reflected changes within South Africa. Since its election the National Party had institutionalized explicitly discriminatory policies, such as the Population Registration Act (1950), the Group Areas Act (1950), the Prohibition of Mixed Marriages Act (1949), and the Immorality Act (1950), followed by the Bantu Education Act (1953) and the Separate Amenities Act (1953). The National Party also consistently expanded the state's coercive apparatus through policies such as the Suppression of Communism Act (1950), the Public Safety Act (1953), the Riotous Assemblies Act (1956), the Unlawful Organizations Act (1956), the Sabotage Act (1962), the Terrorism Act (1967), and the Internal Security Act (1976), all of which gave the police vast powers. Rather than placating South Africa's critics, these policies fueled both domestic and international opposition in the 1950s and beyond.

As UN attention increasingly focused on the broader issues of race relations and universal human rights, the South African claim of domestic jurisdiction was to support.[11] But in the 1950s the United Na-

9. Ibid.

10. T. B. Millar, *The Commonwealth and the United Nations* (London: Methuen, 1967), p. 145.

11. Norms of human rights were defined in the framework of postwar opposition to Nazism and fascism (fundamental in the creation of the United Nations). Many states, especially in the Third World, did not completely accept the Western focus on political or civil rights but rather stressed social and economic rights. John Gerard Ruggie disaggregates the universalist notion of human rights into three subsets: "civil liberties and political rights as they are understood in the West," "economic, social, and cultural rights" (focusing both on East-West and North-South divisions), and the "physical security of the person" ("Human Rights," p. 99). For a contrasting defense of the universality

tions still demonstrated little interest in concrete actions, despite increasing discussions of South African domestic policies. With talk of an International Court of Justice ruling on competence, specific UN resolutions consistently advocated enhancing discussion through noninterventionist steps, such as the establishment of a study commission and reports on progress. Meanwhile, the South African government continued to implement its apartheid policies. Relying on article 2, chapter 7 of the charter, the National Party government consistently rejected discussion of its policies. Although never claiming to approve of apartheid, a number of states supported South Africa's arguments of domestic jurisdiction throughout the 1950s. Substantial disagreement even over the language of resolutions persisted.

By the end of the 1950s, however, language and proposed actions had changed. In 1958, for example, a General Assembly resolution still stated mildly that respect for human rights in a multiracial society is "best assured when patterns of legislation and practice are directed towards ensuring equality before the law of all persons regardless of race, creed, or color, and when the economic, social, cultural, and political participation of all racial groups is on a basis of equality." It also stated that "governmental policies of Member States which are not directed towards these goals, but which are designed to perpetuate or increase discrimination, are inconsistent with the pledges of the Members under Article 56 of the Charter."[12] But just two years later, following the Sharpeville killings, the General Assembly passed Resolution 1598 almost unanimously, collectively rejecting apartheid as "reprehensible and repugnant to human dignity."[13] Subsequent discussions of

---

of the Western conception, see R. J. Vincent, *Human Rights and International Relations* (Cambridge: Cambridge University Press, 1986). Jack Donnelly, in *Universal Human Rights in Theory and Practice* (Ithaca: Cornell University Press, 1989), also defends a universalist conception by rejecting cultural relativism as based on notions of human dignity, not rights.

12. General Assembly Resolution 1248 (XIII), adopted 70-5-4, with Australia, Belgium, France, Portugal, and Britain voting against and the Dominican Republic, Luxembourg, the Netherlands, and Spain abstaining. (Resolutions and votes are summarized in the annual *Yearbook.*) Breaking with its own precedent of abstaining on resolutions and supporting domestic jurisdiction, the United States was instrumental in negotiating a weaker version of the Afro-Asian draft so it could vote with the majority. This shift corresponded with the creation of a separate Bureau of African Affairs within the State Department. On the U.S. position, see the report of the Study Commission on U.S. Policy toward Southern Africa, *South Africa: Time Running Out* (Berkeley: University of California Press, 1981), p. 346.

13. General Assembly Resolution 1598 (XV), passed 93-1-0; Portugal, a colonial power in southern Africa, cast the only negative vote.

apartheid gave increasing consideration to the norm of racial equality within a broadening human rights perspective.

Significant shifts in voting also emerged. The number of abstentions (rather than opposing votes) rose as the appearance of supporting South Africa became unacceptable. Resolutions condemning apartheid and South Africa's failure to respond to UN proposals began to receive unanimous consent.[14] Even the most skeptical members (such as Britain) acknowledged that the problems of apartheid were exceptional.[15] Indeed, as resolutions of condemnation grew more ritualized, South Africa was ever more rarely described without the adjective "racist," and apartheid was declared a "crime against humanity."

Not only did the tone change as racial equality became the predominant norm; the question of appropriate actions arose as several states expressed their frustration at the ineffectiveness of previous UN measures. Resolution 1598, the compromise resolution passed in the aftermath of the Sharpeville killings, "request[ed] all States to consider taking such separate and collective action as is open to them, in conformity with the Charter of the United Nations, to bring about the abandonment of these [apartheid] policies." An even stronger draft resolution "solemnly recommended" that all states consider several more specific measures, including breaking diplomatic relations, closing ports to South African vessels, boycotting imports and exports, and refusing aircraft landing rights.[16] Thus the norm of racial equality prevailed.

The Demise of Domestic Jurisdiction

Following the shock of the Sharpeville killings, support for South Africa's persistent excuses of sovereignty declined. International concern over South African domestic conditions shifted discussion to determining appropriate action, beginning with the initial General Assembly proposal for sanctions. But as its voluntary sanctions resolutions and the condemnation of apartheid failed to be translated into enforced policies, the Security Council became the new center of debate.

Conducting any discussion within the Security Council, however, did not favor those interested in promoting a more active role for the United Nations, because of its different set of procedural norms. The

14. For example, Resolution 1598 (XV), 95-1-0; Resolution 1663 (XVI), 97-2-1; Resolution 1881 (XVIII), 106-1-0; Resolution 1978 (XVIII), 100-2-1. South Africa and Portugal consistently voted against these resolutions.
15. *Yearbook,* 1960, p. 148.
16. Ibid., p. 149.

salient criterion for bringing a matter to the Council is its evaluation as a threat to international peace and security. In addition, the charter granted permanent members (China, France, Britain, the Soviet Union, and the United States) veto power. As a result, proponents of mandatory action had to meet two prerequisites: to get the Security Council to include apartheid as an agenda item, and to prevail on the permanent members not to veto a resolution.

Pressures for Security Council consideration coincided with a dramatic growth in the number of independent African states, whose influence manifested itself both through larger majorities in UN voting and through the increasing articulation of an alternative Pan-Africanist perspective.[17] Particularly for newly independent African states, apartheid (and white minority rule in southern Africa generally) was a vestige of colonialism. In contrast, Western members' concern with racial discrimination was a reaction to Nazism. As more former colonies joined the United Nations, tensions between old and new members escalated.[18] In discussions of apartheid, these tensions were felt in debates over the implications of racial discrimination for conflict in southern Africa.

The Security Council's first consideration of the apartheid issue in 1960 was a dramatic gesture. The Sharpeville killings had demonstrated the ineffectiveness of previous attempts at conciliation and had convinced more conservative governments that some type of international pressure on the South African government might be appropriate. Attention converged on the Council because, unlike the General Assembly, it is empowered by the UN Charter to take action. Some proponents of stronger measures even hoped to establish a precedent for future use of military force.[19]

Although the Security Council accepted apartheid onto its agenda,

17. References here to the Pan-Africanist perspective take Organization of African Unity positions as representative of a general African consensus. Although various divisions exist among African states and not all have acted according to these norms, most students of the OAU note its stress on preserving normative consensus, especially about opposition to apartheid and white minority rule. The Pan-Africanist perspective has been translated into action in different ways, most notably through the formation of the Africa Group caucus within the United Nations and the funding of liberation movements through the Liberation Support Committee. For more on Pan-Africanism and the OAU, see chapter 5 below.

18. Lyons, "In Search of Racial Equality," pp. 75–76; Millar, *Commonwealth*, p. 148; Ali A. Mazrui, *Towards a Pax-Africana: A Study of Ideology and Ambition* (London: Weidenfeld and Nicolson, 1967), p. 132.

19. Millar, *Commonwealth*, pp. 156–57.

the most cautious members considered the South African situation only a *potential* threat to international peace and security. France and Britain, furthermore, had not changed their stance that the matter was outside Council jurisdiction. Its Resolution 134, calling on South Africa to eliminate apartheid, merely expressed concern that South Africa's policies had led to "international friction" and might endanger international peace and security in the future; it did not advocate action.[20] In contrast, African and Asian members believed the situation had grave "potentialities" for international friction that endangered the maintenance of international peace and security. As always, South Africa submitted a lengthy defense based on the idea of domestic jurisdiction.

The Security Council may have been willing to discuss apartheid, but it was far from becoming actively involved in the situation, despite the wishes of the more radical UN members. Nor were members willing to give South Africa much attention after this initial, post-Sharpeville discussion. Nevertheless, the argument for domestic jurisdiction was thereafter severely weakened by the precedent of the Council's consideration. Instead of domestic jurisdiction, the focus of debate was now whether South African policies and actions were a threat to international peace and security.

Different perspectives on the causes of southern African conflict led to different conclusions both about the international implications of apartheid (in part, whether it threatened the peace) and about what types of international pressure might effectively change South African policies. Consensus on condemnation of apartheid was evident by the early 1960s, a major step toward international action, but fundamental differences between the Western powers and the Pan-Africanists remained.[21] These divergent views revealed themselves in the recurring debates over sanctions. Pan-Africanists saw white minority rule as the root cause of southern African problems. Their proposed solution, therefore, was fundamental change in governmental institutions and, above all, majority rule. Alternatively, more conservative governments considered sufficient some type of increased inclusion of blacks into

20. Security Council Resolution 134 (1960), passed 9-0-2; France and Britain abstained on grounds of competence.

21. By this time, the Afro-Asian coalition had also gained the support of the Soviet Union and the Eastern Bloc, as well as China. The stances of Latin American and Western European countries varied. The main focus here, however, is on Britain and the United States, the permanent members most responsible for blocking substantive action.

the political system—short of universal suffrage, and to be implemented gradually.[22]

These divergent interpretations of southern African conflict persisted throughout the ensuing thirty years of debates over anti-apartheid
sanctions. Both views grew more sophisticated as time passed and tur-
moil within South Africa continued, but within the United Nations the
two sides never found enough common ground to develop a consensus
on appropriate action. Consequently, the United Nations adopted
wide-ranging voluntary sanctions but never the comprehensive mandatory economic sanctions that anti-apartheid activists sought.

VOLUNTARY VERSUS MANDATORY SANCTIONS

The United Nations adopted a wide range of diplomatic, economic,
and military sanctions during the 1960s, 1970s, and 1980s. Since these
various voluntary and mandatory measures affected South Africa in different ways, we should distinguish among the types of sanctions in order to assess their impact. It is important not simply to perpetuate
skepticism about the United Nations' failure to adopt comprehensive
mandatory economic sanctions: the United Nations delegitimized
South Africa through diplomatic sanctions, and even the permanent
members of the Security Council adopted a mandatory arms embargo.

Diplomatic Sanctions

As early as 1960, African states agitated for South Africa's exclusion
from various international organizations, reflecting a tactical shift away
from study commissions to sanctions. Several organizations, particularly
those that functioned by majority vote, either completely expelled
South Africa or severely curtailed its participation. The Economic and
Social Council, Economic Commission on Africa, International Labor
Organization, World Health Organization, Food and Agriculture Organization, International Atomic Energy Agency, Universal Postal
Union, and other specialized UN agencies—all restricted South Af-

22. These differences also arose in negotiations over Rhodesian independence
(1965–80). Conservative proposals for constitutional changes allowed some accommodation to African political demands but did not substantially compromise white political
control; these plans included qualified franchise (based upon wealth or education) and
separate houses of parliament (divided along various ethnic or functional lines). For
more on the legacy of the Rhodesia debates, see chapters 4 and 8 below.

rica's membership.[23] South Africa's widespread exclusion marked early success in implementing diplomatic sanctions.

These diplomatic sanctions frequently worked because South Africa's opponents brought the business of these bodies to a standstill until the membership issue was resolved. Debate was often vociferous. Opponents of South Africa's expulsion based their objections primarily on the principle of universality of membership whereas proponents of exclusion sought to decrease international recognition of the National Party government while recognizing, and supporting, the liberation movements as legitimate representatives of the South African people.[24] Thus the African National Congress (ANC) and Pan-African Congress gained official status, and access to various bureaucrats and diplomats.

However, permanent members prevented South Africa's expulsion from the United Nations, underscoring the difference between majority opinion in the Assembly and action controlled by the Council. Similarly, South Africa's opponents failed to restrict its access to international loans through the World Bank and the International Monetary Fund. Dominated by Western governments, these organizations insisted on established financial standards of membership, and countries could be excluded only if they had not fulfilled their financial obligations.[25] Thus in these arenas, functional norms prevailed.

Despite South Africa's continued access to international finance and formal United Nations membership, the scope of its diplomatic exclusion was extraordinary. African states and their Third World allies established near-universal rhetorical and diplomatic opposition to South African apartheid, reflected in the rapid passage of numerous voluntary sanctions. However, this broad symbolic consensus supporting a norm of racial equality did not automatically lead to further actions after the strategy of diplomatic isolation reached its limits. Western powers stymied other types of sanctions.[26] By the mid-1960s, a second strategy

23. On the debates in these organizations, see Richard E. Bissell, *Apartheid and International Organizations* (Boulder, Colo.: Westview Press, 1977), esp. pp. 80–95.

24. Despite both its minimal participation and the government's isolationist perspective, South Africa did not withdraw. One possible explanation is that it hoped to forestall use of the United Nations as a means of recognizing an opposition government-in-exile. See John Barratt, "South African Diplomacy at the UN," in *Diplomacy at the UN*, ed. G. R. Berridge and A. Jennings (New York: St. Martin's, 1985), esp. pp. 198–202.

25. Bissell, *Apartheid*, p. 117.

26. General Assembly resolutions received only bland Western concurrence, encouraging states to (voluntarily) take separate and collective action to bring about the abandonment of apartheid. For example, Resolution 1663 (XVI) in 1961 was adopted by a nearly unanimous vote of 97-2-1 (Portugal and South Africa against, Guinea abstaining).

[handwritten marginalia: use of int'l inst'l to legitimize]

therefore developed: the expansion of informational activities through the Special Committee on Apartheid (established in 1964).[27] Anti-apartheid activists succeeded in using the UN structure to legitimize the liberation movements of southern Africa.

Military Sanctions

In 1977 the Security Council passed Resolution 418 (with no absten-tions). This mandatory arms embargo was the only mandatory sanctions package that the permanent members adopted. But rather than mark-ing a substantial policy change (as sanctions proponents had hoped), the Council's decision reflected circumstantial changes in regional pol-itics, as is evident from a comparison of the 1977 mandatory embargo and the 1963 voluntary embargo.

In 1963 the Security Council passed Resolution 181 (with Britain and France abstaining) in response to concerns that some of the arms in South Africa's recent build-up were being used "in furtherance of that Government's racial policies" and that "some States are indirectly providing encouragement . . . to the Government of South Africa to perpetuate, by force, its policy of apartheid." Council members noted that "the situation in South Africa is seriously disturbing the interna-tional peace and security" and called both for South Africa to abandon its apartheid policy and for other states to cease arms sales.

In contrast to its later support for the mandatory embargo in 1977, Britain abstained on these voluntary sanctions, declaring that it "would not interfere with the sale and shipment of equipment to be used by South Africa in making and maintaining arms against external attack and reserved their right to fulfil existing contracts with South Africa."[28] The United States was concerned about what types of arms qualified for the 1963 restrictions, and the Western powers generally justified arms sales on the grounds of the right to self-defense. For example, when the conservative Heath government announced its intention to sell arms to South Africa in 1971, it claimed that weapons such as battleships could not be used for internal repression (intense Com-monwealth pressure reversed the policy).

In 1977, the Western powers still rejected any fundamental relation-ship between South Africa's external and internal policies. Although

27. On UN support to the liberation movements, see Wellington Nyangoni, *Africa in the United Nations System* (Washington, D.C.: Associated University Press, 1985).

28. *Yearbook*, 1963, p. 18.

condemning apartheid and domestic violence in South Africa (notably in Resolution 417, adopted just days before the arms embargo), Security Council members cited South Africa's increasingly confrontational foreign policy, not internal repression, as the reason for the escalating regional conflict.[29] Britain concluded that "the acquisition by South Africa of arms and related material in the current situation constituted a threat to the maintenance of international peace and security," even though it still opposed isolation as a general response to apartheid.[30] The United States was dissatisfied with the ineffectiveness of the voluntary embargo, and expressed concern over the possibility of South Africa's acquiring a nuclear capability.[31] Further indicating that the 1977 arms embargo was not directed at apartheid per se, Western powers simultaneously decided against mandatory economic sanctions. Canada, France, West Germany, Britain, and the United States all rejected a draft resolution that declared that the policies and actions of the South African regime constituted a grave threat to international peace and security, as well as other drafts invoking restrictions on loans and stronger restrictions on arms trade.[32]

The 1976 Soweto riots may have been partly responsible for provoking the UN arms embargo, but domestic unrest does not convincingly explain the permanent members' decisions. Rather, regional changes, including South Africa's overt military involvement in neighboring states (especially Angola in 1975), the general escalation of the Rhodesian war (in which South Africa was also indirectly involved), and the perception of guerrilla forces and new governments as being inspired and supported by communists, provoked Western powers' action. The 1977 mandatory arms embargo was an anomaly among the array of sanctions against South Africa.

---

29. African states had consistently argued that apartheid was a continental problem. Only in the later 1970s did South Africa's foreign policy become overtly aggressive and threaten the sovereignty of neighboring states as it developed its concept of "total strategy." Previously, it had pursued an "outward-looking policy" of attempting to diminish its isolation by promoting "dialogue" with African states. On South Africa's policies and the African response, see Barber and Barratt, *South Africa's Foreign Policy*, and chapter 5 below.

30. The British representative added, "It would be naive, however, to believe that complex negotiations on the peaceful, democratic transition to independence elsewhere in southern Africa could take place in a situation where South Africa had decided to isolate itself totally from the international community" (*Yearbook*, 1977, p. 143).

31. Ibid. This shift in U.S. policy coincided with the human rights emphasis of the early Carter administration. It did not, however, result in support for economic sanctions (see chapter 6 below).

32. Ibid., pp. 137–47.

Economic Sanctions

The Western powers' rejection of economic sanctions continued substantially unchanged through the 1980s, even as the 1984–86 riots and states of emergency received international condemnation comparable to what followed the 1976 Soweto riots. South Africa simultaneously pursued an aggressive foreign policy, including armed raids on neighboring states and support for armed rebel movements, commonly known as "destabilization." A series of Security Council draft resolutions in favor of stricter sanctions (usually comprehensive mandatory economic sanctions) reached the voting stage in the mid-1980s, only to be rejected by Western powers.

Between 1985 and 1987, the United States rejected mandatory measures, arguing that severing economic ties would lead to more bloodshed in South Africa while depriving the international community of any leverage. Similarly, Britain argued that sanctions would undermine its attempts to promote dialogue. France, although acknowledging the need to pressure the South African government, expressed reservations about the appropriateness of sanctions. The same countries also consistently vetoed draft resolutions calling for sanctions against South Africa owing to its refusal to grant independence to Namibia.[33]

At the heart of these disagreements between African and Western perspectives on sanctions lay complex political questions, particularly about whether apartheid could be reformed and whether South African leaders were willing to compromise. Those most in favor of broad and mandatory sanctions (the Pan-Africanists) also advocated substantial structural changes, far beyond the removal of overt racial discrimination. Opponents of sanctions (the Western powers) generally promoted gradual transformation, often citing the benefits of overall economic growth for removing "inefficiencies" derived from racial segregation and discrimination. Supporters of strong external action, at a minimum comprehensive mandatory sanctions, saw violence within South Africa as an outcome of the apartheid system. Others, such as the National Party government, saw the violence of protest as the result of agitators (in their words, "communists" or "terrorists"). Those who perceived violence as endemic to the system more often sympathized with armed struggle as a reaction to that violence, whereas others, argu-

33. United Nations, Office of Public Information, *UN Chronicle* 23 (August 1986), 29–32; *UN Chronicle* 24 (May 1987), 22–23; *UN Chronicle* 24 (August 1987), 22–25. For a typical resolution of this period, see Security Council Resolution 581 (1986).

ing that the imposition of sanctions would increase domestic unrest, rejected armed struggle as illegitimate.

These interrelated issues defined the boundaries of the debates over sanctions from the 1960s through the late 1980s; polarization marked the debates of the mid-1980s. Yet the other successes of three decades of anti-apartheid activism in the United Nations are striking, such as recognition of the liberation movement (including persistent attention drawn to the imprisoned ANC leader Nelson Mandela), and considerable humanitarian, social, economic, technical, and educational aid.[34] Thus despite their failure to achieve their proclaimed goal of comprehensive mandatory economic sanctions against South Africa, activists successfully used the UN system to strengthen global opposition to apartheid.

In sum, within the United Nations, a norm of racial equality acquired universal acceptance and codification, while apartheid discrimination received persistent, protracted condemnation. Following global decolonization, the UN General Assembly became the primary forum for criticizing South Africa, and adopting voluntary sanctions ranging from diplomatic exclusion in affiliated organizations to arms boycotts. Yet South Africa's isolation by the 1960s belies the lack of stronger economic measures in the 1970s and 1980s. Third World pressure succeeded in organizational settings where majority voting prevailed, but not in the Security Council, where Western permanent members vetoed comprehensive mandatory sanctions. Nevertheless, UN activities substantially benefited the anti-apartheid movement. Institutional changes incorporated South African liberation movements, granting legitimacy and providing crucial financial assistance. The information battle to publicize apartheid and to isolate South Africa continued. With UN support, exiled South Africans sustained their opposition during decades of severe domestic repression.

South Africa's isolation within the United Nations system demonstrates the agenda-setting power of the anti-apartheid movement and counters conventional theories that stress coercive power alone. For example, procedural norms, such as majority versus veto, bolstered the

---

34. Newell M. Stultz argues against the stalemate perspective; see "The Apartheid Issue at the General Assembly: Stalemate or Gathering Storm?" *African Affairs* 86 (January 1987), 25–37. Although correctly stressing educational and informational work, Stultz overemphasizes the importance of quantitative changes in UN voting patterns and characteristics of anti-apartheid resolutions.

influence of—and set limitations on—African states. However, a neoliberal institutionalist focus on rules and incentives leaves many un-
answered questions about the nature of the costs and benefits of racial
equality. Not all norms have value that can be easily translated into
market considerations. The experience of sanctions advocates supports
general institutionalist claims and points especially to the role of norms
in legitimation.

UN sanctions against South Africa therefore call into question the
foundation of conventional sanctions analyses. Because of their acceptance of realist theories, which minimize the importance of norms and
institutions, most sanctions analysts reach pessimistic conclusions. By
assuming that sanctions are an alternative to military force, they maintain the realist focus on coercive capabilities. In addition, by asserting
that economic sanctions need to be comprehensive and mandatory,
they perpetuate the realist belief that only the threat of overwhelming
economic costs (comparable to the costs of war) will coerce the compliance of a target state. Finally, by dismissing diplomatic sanctions as
symbolic and superficial, conventional sanctions analysts reproduce the
realist dismissal of legitimation effects. Conventional analyses, in other
words, miss a crucial point, that South Africa's domestic discrimination
conflicted with prevailing global norms, and that as a result almost all
states responded with some form of sanctions.

CHAPTER FOUR

The Commonwealth

As an informal grouping of Britain and its former colonies, the Commonwealth offers both theoretical and practical contrasts to the United Nations. Its consensus-based decision making and off-the-record summit meetings foster compromise, unlike the majority voting and veto procedures of most other formal organizations. In addition, sanctions analysts are well versed in UN policies and procedures but rarely examine the Commonwealth (except for a few cases, notably Rhodesia and South Africa). Realists might well assume that Commonwealth policies should follow the British lead because of the group's origins in empire and the absence of empowering procedural norms such as majority voting. The Commonwealth's adoption in the mid-1980s of sanctions that Britain resisted is an anomaly for conventional sanctions analyses.

Nor does regime theory's focus on functional norms and cost-benefit calculation explain Commonwealth politics. Neoliberal institutionalists cannot explain Britain's failure to control the South Africa issue, especially in the early 1960s, when it most clearly dominated the informal organization. As in the United Nations, a broad coalition of African and Asian members advocated sanctions against South Africa in the face of Britain's opposition. Despite the lack of substantial material gains from its Commonwealth ties and the group's continuing condemnation of its opposition to sanctions, Britain nonetheless stayed within the Commonwealth. The costs and benefits of racial equality remain incalculable, but Commonwealth policies toward South Africa do prove the intangible value of group identity through membership in international associations.

Anti-apartheid activists' success, both in excluding South Africa from the Commonwealth in 1961 and in generating multilateral sanctions in the mid-1980s, demonstrates the power of a norm of racial equality for motivating and coordinating multilateral policies. In the first section of this chapter, I examine South Africa's withdrawal from the Commonwealth and subsequent organizational changes, arguing that South Africa's exclusion and Britain's declining hegemony both resulted from the increasing strength of this norm. In the second section, on the sanctions debates of the mid-1980s, I argue that Commonwealth perspectives on both regionalism and reform resulted from the dominance of a Pan-African perspective on racial equality. Commonwealth sanctions show the capacity of a norm to define countries' collective identity and coordinate their policies.

RACIAL EQUALITY REDEFINES COMMUNITY

The Commonwealth states' special relationship derives from their common history of British colonialism. Until the Second World War, the member states' sovereignty evolved gradually, with the devolution of authority over domestic affairs preceding that over defense policy. Later, however, in contrast to this trend toward formal sovereignty, the advocates of racial equality challenged South Africa's domestic segregation as well as its membership within the Commonwealth, resulting in the redefinition of the group's collective identity, both in principle and in organizational form.

South African Withdrawal

For Australia, Canada, Ireland, South Africa, and New Zealand, demands for increased autonomy (particularly spurred by the issue of providing troops to fight in two world wars) resulted in the evolution of Dominion status within the British Empire. Variations in the degree of Dominion autonomy stemmed from each country's specific political, cultural, economic, and strategic situations; Canada, Ireland, and South Africa were most interested in substantial autonomy.[1] But despite

---

1. Much has been written to explain why the Commonwealth persisted despite pressures for autonomy, ranging from interest theories to idealist notions focusing on the British political heritage and the symbolism of the Crown. For a sampling, see J. D. B.

these pressures for decentralization, the Commonwealth continued to revolve around Britain, with direct relations among the Dominions playing a more minor role.

Dynamics within the Commonwealth changed dramatically after the Second World War, starting with the independence of India. Neither a Dominion nor a typical Third World colony, India's new status as a sovereign republic within the Commonwealth presented a unique compromise, altering the previous constitutional requirement that the British monarch remain the head of state in all Dominions. India's membership called into question constitutive assumptions of the commonality of British political ancestry and thus started the transformation from an Anglo to a multiracial Commonwealth. As decolonization proceeded beyond Indian independence, the Commonwealth expanded to incorporate former colonies that had also declared their independence from the Crown.[2]

Former colonies were not the only governments interested in attaining republican status within the Commonwealth; South Africa's National Party also wanted increased autonomy from Britain.[3] But South Africa was the only Dominion wanting both to establish republican sta-

---

Miller, *The Commonwealth in the World* (London: Gerard Duckworth, 1958); M. Margaret Ball, *The "Open" Commonwealth* (Durham, N.C.: Duke University Press, 1971); Derek Ingram, *The Imperfect Commonwealth* (London: Rex Collings, 1977); W. C. B. Tunstall, *The Commonwealth and Regional Defense* (London: Athlone, 1959); and J. D. B. Miller, *Survey of Commonwealth Affairs: Problems of Expansion and Attrition, 1953–1969* (London: Oxford University Press, 1974).

2. Although the early Commonwealth was often referred to as a "white club," race seems to have been more of an implicit influence, with notions of a common British heritage being more explicitly acknowledged (although the two are not entirely distinct, as race can play a large part in defining that culture). Not surprisingly, Dominion demands for autonomy differed qualitatively from those of the non-European colonies; see Nicholas Mansergh, *The Commonwealth Experience*, Vol. 2, *From British to Multiracial Commonwealth*, rev. ed. (Toronto: University of Toronto Press, 1982). For the African perspective on, and increased role in, the Commonwealth, see Ali A. Mazrui, *The Anglo-African Commonwealth: Political Friction and Cultural Fusion* (London: Pergamon, 1967). Many participants and observers of the "new" Commonwealth still emphasize the common heritage, with attention now primarily upon the parliamentary (legal) tradition and the shared use of the English language.

3. Afrikaners were never willing members of the British Empire (as evident from the Boer wars) but had been incorporated into the Commonwealth through the Union of South Africa, which was established in 1910. An Afrikaner politician's views on the Republican issue had significant career implications. Fellow Afrikaners criticized Jan Smuts for his faith in the British Empire. D. F. Malan, the first National Party prime minister and architect of apartheid, also came under criticism for his change in attitude towards the Commonwealth; see O. Geyser, "A Commonwealth Prime Minister: D. F. Malan 1948–54," *The Round Table* 307 (July 1988), 307–11.

tus and to retain Commonwealth membership, thus creating a procedural anomaly (in contrast, Ireland became a republic and left the Commonwealth). Setting the stage for contentious debate, members decided that after becoming a republic, South Africa would have to apply anew for membership. Since there were no procedures for expelling a member, South Africa's critics took this opportunity to challenge its nominal reentry on grounds that its racial policies were incompatible with the principles of the emerging multiracial Commonwealth. This challenge reflected the fundamental objections to white minority rule held by members of an increasingly multiracial organization, and the belief of many members that domestic policies based on racial discrimination were incompatible with the (implicit) principles of the Commonwealth.[4] As in the United Nations, Pan-Africanists argued that white rule in South Africa was both a form of colonial rule and a threat to racial equality. Tanganyika's Julius Nyerere argued, "In our struggle for self-government and independence we have spoken of brotherhood and the equality of man. . . . The apartheid policies now being practiced in the Union of South Africa are a daily affront to this belief in human dignity. They are also a constantly reiterated insult to our own dignity as Africans."[5]

Initially, South Africa adamantly attempted to keep discussion of apartheid off the Commonwealth agenda, arguing that its domestic policies had no bearing on membership. As in the United Nations, South Africa here defended its international status by invoking the established norm of domestic jurisdiction.[6] At the 1960 summit meeting, which took place one month after the Sharpeville shootings, South Africa sought approval for continued membership before its own referendum on the republic issue. Under pressure, its representative (Minister

4. A secondary issue was that of diplomatic representation in South Africa by Africans from independent states who, South Africa reaffirmed, would be subject to the same discriminatory legislation as South Africans.

5. Quoted in J. D. B. Miller, "South Africa's Departure," *Journal of Commonwealth Political Studies* 1 (November 1961), 72–73.

6. Before 1960, the norm of noninterference in domestic affairs was firmly established within the Commonwealth, having been emphasized by Britain since 1926 and recognized by the Statute of Westminster in 1931. On the shift from norms of noninterference to multiracialism, see R. H. Wagenberg, "Commonwealth Reactions to South Africa's Racial Policy 1948–1961" (Diss., London School of Economics, 1966). Distinctions between domestic and international concerns are inherently less clear within the Commonwealth than in other international organizations, since, prior to republican membership, its component countries did not have clearly defined sovereignty, nor did they explicitly choose to become members. Also, the Commonwealth has no charter or other formal constitutional structure that would define such distinctions.

of External Affairs Louw) agreed to informal discussions of his country's policies. Consensus developed that South Africa would indeed have to apply for readmission if white South Africans passed the referendum. The final communiqué, issued after the summit, reaffirmed domestic jurisdiction but conveyed members' commitment to ensuring good relations within the "multiracial association."[7] A crisis was thus deferred until the next summit meeting in March 1961.

After South Africa declared its intention to adopt a republican constitution, and despite British and Australian sympathy for the argument of domestic jurisdiction, the Heads of Government meeting reconsidered the membership issue. Although there had never been a unanimous push to expel South Africa, several members, particularly some newly and soon-to-be independent African states, refused to participate within the Commonwealth if South Africa remained a member.[8] Nor was South Africa willing to compromise to avoid a break.

With these two incompatible positions confronting the Commonwealth, Canada unexpectedly stepped in to mediate the conflict between the principles of nonintervention and multiracialism. Canada attempted to gain concessions from South Africa, rather than backing either the noninterference principle or the separation of racial and constitutional issues (the alternative compromise that Britain and Australia favored).[9] The decisive views of Canadian prime minister John Diefenbaker bridged the white Dominion (and British) position and the African-Asian position, thereby preventing a racial alignment and the breakup of the organization. Diefenbaker consistently insisted on the need to recognize the multiracial character of the Commonwealth by not automatically accepting South Africa's readmission. Yet he also would have accepted even minor symbolic concessions from South Af-

7. Final Communiqué, Meeting of Commonwealth Prime Ministers, 1960, reproduced in *The Commonwealth at the Summit* (London: Commonwealth Secretariat, 1987), p. 63. Unless otherwise noted, all further communiqués mentioned here can be found in this compendium and will simply be cited in the text by year.

8. During the meeting, Nyerere published an editorial in the London *Observer* (12 March 1961) in which he announced that Tanganyika would not join the Commonwealth if South Africa remained, because "neutrality is not possible." "By refusing to join," he continued, "we should be making clear that we are prepared to do anything which is necessary to protect our society from spiritual as well as material evil. . . . to vote for South Africa is to vote us out." The article reportedly affected the debates within the meeting; see Miller, "South Africa's Departure," pp. 61–62 and 72–74.

9. Nehru (India), Nkrumah (Ghana), and Diefenbaker (Canada) were crucial in preventing this separation of issues (see Miller, *Survey*, p. 155).

rica.[10] Such a compromise, however, was forestalled by South African intransigence, including its refusal to approve a final communiqué critical of its policies.[11] This consistent inflexibility (maintained by both Foreign Minister Louw in 1960 and Prime Minister Verwoerd in 1961) provoked increased criticism.

By forcing South Africa to choose between acknowledging the principle of racial equality and withdrawing from the organization, the prime ministers averted a final decision between readmittance or expulsion. The evolving discussions during the 1961 meeting converged around the possibility of framing a statement of Commonwealth principles—containing a commitment to racial equality—whose acceptance would be a condition of membership. Even British prime minister Macmillan, chairman of the meeting, acknowledged the need to establish Commonwealth principles after it became apparent that he would not be able to mobilize a consensus to separate the constitutional and racial issues. Advocates for racial equality as a fundamental principle of the organization prevailed. South Africa withdrew its request for readmission to the Commonwealth.

The final communiqué of the first prime ministers' meeting (in 1962) after South African withdrawal characterized "race relations" as one of the major issues of the day, acknowledging the Commonwealth's potential for "cooperation among peoples of several races and continents" and "constructive leadership in the application of democratic principles." Reaffirming their commitment to racial equality and international cooperation in the Declaration of Commonwealth Principles (adopted 22 January 1971 at the Singapore summit), member states opposed racism as "an unmitigated evil" and declared that "no country will afford to regimes which practice racial discrimination assistance which in its own judgement directly contributes to the pursuit or consolidation of this evil policy." In principle, members of the Common-

10. H. Basil Robinson, *Diefenbaker's World: A Populist in Foreign Affairs* (Toronto: University of Toronto Press, 1989), p. 174. Diefenbaker also did not want to take sole responsibility for denying South Africa membership. It is important to note the moderate tone of these meetings. Some type of token compromise would probably have satisfied many critics besides Diefenbaker, particularly at the 1960 meeting.

11. See Miller, *Survey*, pp. 127–66, and James Barber and John Barratt, *South Africa's Foreign Policy: The Search for Status and Security 1945–1988* (Cambridge: Cambridge University Press, 1990), pp. 81–83. South Africa's only attempt at compromise was to suggest that it would agree to one of Britain's draft communiqués (which contained criticisms of apartheid), but only on the condition that it could also present its views at length. The group rejected this alternative, arguing that it would allot too much attention to South Africa's views.

wealth committed themselves to racial equality; its implementation remained to be seen.

Institutional Transformation

The constitutive character and institutional structures of this new multiracial Commonwealth evolved as conflicts over racial equality persisted. Southern African issues remained the driving force behind fundamental transformation in the Commonwealth's character and structure, despite South Africa's preemptive withdrawal. In particular, conflicts over Rhodesian independence (1965–80) substantially affected the distribution of power within the association, strengthening its nascent secretariat and weakening British hegemony. The African-Asian majority emerged decisive.

The Commonwealth served as an arena where the African-Asian majority consistently articulated the goal of increased African representation in Rhodesia and South Africa. Prior to the Rhodesian Front's Unilateral Declaration of Independence on 11 November 1965, African and Asian members urged Britain not to grant independence to Prime Minister Ian Smith's self-governing, colonial regime under a constitution that preserved white minority rule. Their pressure for a commitment to majority rule was partially responsible for Britain's refusal to grant independence to (Southern) Rhodesia under a white minority regime at the same time as its other central African colonies, Northern Rhodesia (now Zambia) and Nyasaland (now Malawi), gained independence with majority rule. And certainly the prior rejection of South African membership had established the notion that minority governments of newly independent states would be severely scrutinized. After UDI, the African and Asian countries pressured Britain to take strong action against the Smith regime; some even called for the use of force.[12]

The creation of a secretariat in July 1965 enhanced African influence in the Commonwealth, further eroding British dominance. Although granting the secretariat only minimal powers, the Heads of Government agreement was vague enough to allow the personality of the secretary-general to mold the direction of the office. The first secre-

12. For a detailed discussion of the issues surrounding Rhodesian independence, see Kenneth Young, *Rhodesia and Independence A Study in British Colonial Policy* (London: J. M. Dent, 1967). For select documentation, see Elaine Windrich, *The Rhodesian Problem: A Documentary Record, 1923–1973* (London: Routledge and Kegan Paul, 1975).

tary-general, Canadian Arnold Smith, spent considerable energy at the beginning of his tenure in establishing his independence from Britain and its Foreign Office. When African countries such as Tanzania and Ghana broke diplomatic relations with Britain over the issue of Rhodesia, Arnold Smith mediated to keep them from withdrawing (and they eventually reestablished official ties with Britain).[13]

The conflict over acceptable constitutional proposals dragged on. Majority rule became a principle clearly articulated in the communiqués from the Commonwealth prime ministers' meetings of this period. Discussing Rhodesia's constitutional structure, the ministers, who in 1964 started out tolerating "sufficiently representative institutions" and independence within the Commonwealth on the basis of eventual majority rule, by 1965 were emphasizing the need for "unimpeded progress to majority rule."[14] Concern crystallized around the more demanding principle of "no independence before majority (African) rule" by 1969. In addition, advocates of racial equality criticized South Africa for economically and militarily supporting the rebel Rhodesian regime.

These southern African issues played a smaller part in Commonwealth debates of the 1970s, but major organizational changes during that decade held significant implications for later debates. By the 1970s, the secretariat had become an independent authority, and the second secretary-general, Shridath Ramphal of Guyana, established a more interventionist leadership style. Ramphal took a more partisan position, particularly on southern African issues, and was known to be a strong advocate of sanctions against South Africa, as well as of a majority rule settlement for Rhodesia.[15] Ramphal's role was crucial in inde-

13. Arnold Smith with Clyde Sanger, *Stitches in Time: The Commonwealth in World Politics* (London: Andre Deutsch, 1981). Summit meetings began to be held in variable locations (the first being Lagos, Nigeria, in 1966 to discuss Rhodesia), another reflection of the decreasing centrality of Britain. Also see Robert Good, *UDI: The International Politics of the Rhodesian Rebellion* (Princeton: Princeton University Press, 1973). For a view of the secretariat rooted in the British foreign service perspective, see Joe Garner, *The Commonwealth Office 1925–68* (London: Heinemann, 1978).

14. Britain maintained that Rhodesian independence was solely a matter of British jurisdiction; their position shifted after UDI as Wilson promoted UN sanctions.

15. Differences over the years in the secretary-general's *Report to the Heads of Government* (London: Commonwealth Secretariat, biennial) manifest these changes from the Smith to Ramphal eras. For his views on southern Africa and sanctions, see Shridath Ramphal, *Inseparable Humanity* (London: Hansib, 1988). For an overview of the role of the secretariat, see Margaret Doxey, *The Commonwealth Secretariat and the Contemporary Commonwealth* (London: Macmillan, 1989).

individual

pendence negotiations, especially in influencing the positions of the Zimbabwean liberation movements.[16]

The Commonwealth's commitment to the principle of no independence before majority rule was evident in the final showdown at the 1979 summit meeting in Lusaka, Zambia, and the subsequent Lancaster House Conference. Because she was willing to grant recognition to Rhodesia, the new British prime minister, Margaret Thatcher, came under concerted pressure at Lusaka from Commonwealth members (including Prime Minister Malcolm Fraser of Australia) and the secretary-general. The outcome was an agreement to hold one more constitutional conference, eventually leading to the Lancaster House Constitution for Zimbabwe, which was based on the principle of universal suffrage.

Thus the issue of the Rhodesian conflict helped shape the transformation of the principle of multiracialism into policy decisions and criteria for an acceptable settlement, with lasting influence on the Commonwealth's norms and institutions, as well as on its policies toward South Africa. The secretariat offered more opportunities not only for African and Asian issues to dominate the agenda but also for the Dominions to play a mediating role between Britain and more radical members. Ramphal also maintained a high profile during the sanctions debates of the 1980s, in which these trends of the 1960s and 1970s were to reach full force.

MULTILATERAL POLICY COORDINATION

The Commonwealth's role in the Rhodesian negotiations translated a commitment to racial equality into criteria for universal suffrage. It also empowered South Africa's opponents, as became evident in the subsequent deliberations over anti-apartheid sanctions. Important new actors had appeared on the scene: the secretary-general and the informal alliance of southern African states known as the Frontline States. Furthermore, a regionalist perspective on the causes of conflict and on

16. Despite other differences in opinion, a wide range of observers and participants acknowledge Ramphal's role. See variously Peter Carrington, *Reflections on Things Past: The Memoirs of Lord Carrington* (London: Collins, 1988); Anthony Verrier, *The Road to Zimbabwe 1890–1980* (London: Jonathan Cape, 1986); Jeffrey Davidow, *A Peace in Southern Africa: The Lancaster House Conference on Rhodesia, 1979* (Boulder, Colo.: Westview Press, 1984); and Margaret Thatcher, *The Downing Street Years* (New York: HarperCollins, 1993), pp. 72–78.

63

the relationship between sanctions and reform became predominant. Based on this general consensus, the Commonwealth policy on sanctions included specific criteria for progress toward negotiated settlement in South Africa and support for its neighboring states. While neither comprehensive nor mandatory, Commonwealth sanctions clearly demonstrated mutual accommodation among its members and sent a strong signal to South Africa that the costs of maintaining apartheid would only increase.

Regionalism and Sanctions

One legacy of the Rhodesian experience for debates over South Africa was the prevalence within the Commonwealth of the Pan-African regionalist perspective, as embodied in and advocated by the Frontline States. As an informal consultative group, the FLS members initially comprised states neighboring Rhodesia or offering bases and assistance to its liberation movements: Angola, Botswana, Mozambique, Tanzania, and Zambia.[17] By the mid-1970s, these five states had become a recognized force in any negotiations on Rhodesia. Their influence caused other Commonwealth members to acknowledge South Africa as a matter of regional, and hence international, concern. The Frontline States were vocal proponents of racial equality and sanctions against South Africa.

Echoing the 1971 Declaration of Commonwealth Principles, the 1979 Lusaka Declaration of the Commonwealth on Racism and Racial Prejudice acknowledged a "responsibility to work together for the total eradication of apartheid and racial discrimination." In 1981, members acknowledged a need to adopt (unspecified) "effective measures" to fight the "evil of apartheid." Although general and vague, such statements during the years leading up to the 1985 summit in Nassau, Bahamas, laid a foundation for an emerging consensus within the Commonwealth on a number of aspects of the southern African situation.

In the communiqués of the early 1980s, the Heads of Government

17. For a more detailed discussion of the origins of this African regional perspective and the Frontline States, see chapter 5 below. Although not neighboring on Rhodesia, Tanzania was the first country, under the auspices of the OAU, to offer bases to the liberation movements. Botswana never offered direct military support but became a home for refugees. Botswana, Tanzania, and Zambia (later to be joined by independent Zimbabwe as a Frontline State) are all Commonwealth members; Angola and Mozambique, former Portuguese colonies, are not.

of Commonwealth members acknowledged South Africa's white minority rule as the root cause of a variety of problems in southern Africa, including internal repression, the delay in independence for Namibia, the destabilization of neighboring countries (including the presence of troops in Angola), and repeated military threats to and violations of their territorial integrity. These leaders viewed such conditions as a threat to regional stability and as a danger to international peace and security. In 1981 they acknowledged the "solemn and urgent duty" of each government to take measures to combat apartheid. Two years later, in 1983, members reiterated their concern over South Africa's repeated violations of neighboring territories and the costs of destabilization among the FLS. They expressed their belief that "the international community as a whole had an obligation to take effective measures to impose restraint on South Africa, and to ensure that the stability of the region was not jeopardized by further acts of aggression." The Commonwealth lauded regional responses to South African policy, such as the promotion of the Southern African Development Coordination Conference, commonly known as SADCC, which attempted to reduce the economic dependence of southern African member states on South Africa.[18]

As a response to increasing regional conflict, the Commonwealth first seriously debated economic sanctions against South Africa in the mid-1980s. Previous (voluntary) sanctions against arms and sporting contacts had been declared in the 1977 Gleneagles Agreement. Widespread popular protests against the Commonwealth Games and sports team tours to South Africa directed considerable public attention to the issue of apartheid. Commonwealth countries also called for more effective implementation of the international arms embargo. At the Nassau meeting in 1985, the Commonwealth targeted South Africa by adopting restrictions on new loans, imports of Krugerrands (gold coins), funding of trade missions, sales of computer equipment to its military or police, exports of oil and arms, and military cooperation. These sanctions, they hoped, would impress upon the South African government the "urgency of dismantling apartheid and erecting the structures of democracy."

Regionalism and recognition of the need for concrete support to

18. Such support coincided with the Commonwealth's emphasis on technical aid and cooperation, as well as increasing support for efforts at regional development schemes throughout the world. For a detailed discussion of the Conference and the costs of destabilization, see chapter 5 below.

South Africa's neighbors were further evident in, and reinforced by, acknowledgement of the Frontline States' need for substantial aid if they were to implement the Commonwealth's package of economic sanctions. For example, the 1986 communiqué, which declared additional sanctions including restrictions on air links and new investment, announced that "as a further element of our collective commitment to effective action, we have requested the Secretary-General, with assistance from our Governments, to co-ordinate the implementation of the agreed measures and to identify such adjustment as may be necessary in Commonwealth countries affected by them." Indeed, discussions of the costs to neighboring states of the international implementation of sanctions became a key issue in the controversy.

Africans hopeful of compensation were disappointed. The Frontline States argued that these costs were regrettable but necessary for eliminating a costlier and longer-term evil, that of white minority rule in South Africa. The Dominions were sympathetic to the FLS position at the height of the sanctions controversy, but Britain clearly stated that it would not support the Frontline States if they chose to implement Commonwealth sanctions. By the 1987 summit, however, even Prime Minister Thatcher supported (military) aid to those states as an alternative to sanctions, thus demonstrating one of the indirect—and unanticipated—consequences of the pressure for sanctions.[19]

The predominant regionalist perspective also became institutionalized within the Commonwealth structure. In particular, the Committee of Foreign Ministers on Southern Africa evolved into the central forum for debates over sanctions.[20] The committee, established in 1985 to evaluate the progress of sanctions, comprised the major actors concerned with southern African issues, notably Canada, Australia, Zambia, and Zimbabwe, in addition to Britain, India, and the Bahamas (as the host country of that summit). The key role the Frontline States had

19. *Globe and Mail* (Toronto), 19 October 1987. In contrast to Thatcher's initial rejection of aid to the Frontline States, other British policies demonstrate the extent to which the regionalist perspective permeated Commonwealth discussions and policy making. For example, Britain gave bilateral military aid to Mozambique; Mozambique became an observer at Commonwealth meetings; and the group established a special fund for aid to Mozambique. One significant aspect of the regionalist perspective confirmed by the British relationship to Mozambique was the redefinition of South Africa into an issue of security, as well as of racial equality. On British policy, also see chapter 7 below.

20. Britain, however, did not support this institutionalization, which further weakened its position and strengthened Australia, Canada, and the Frontline States. See in particular David R. Black, "Middle Power Diplomacy and the Pursuit of Change in South Africa: Canada, Australia, and the Commonwealth Committee of Foreign Ministers on Southern Africa" (paper presented at the annual meeting of the International Studies Association, Vancouver, Canada, April 1991).

played was perpetuated by this subsidiary organization, which increasingly became responsible for articulating a Commonwealth position. The committee also commissioned a number of important studies that monitored the effects of sanctions and shaped the agenda for the future direction of economic pressures, particularly the emerging attention to international finance.[21]

Sanctions and Reform

The Commonwealth's anti-apartheid efforts focused on fostering negotiations in South Africa. The initial 1985 Nassau sanctions package included a set of conditions that the Heads of Government saw as conducive to successful dialogue and which they established as prerequisites for the lifting of those sanctions. As defined in the 1985 Commonwealth Accord on Southern Africa, these prerequisites were that South Africa:

(1) declare that the system of apartheid would be dismantled and take specific and meaningful action in fulfillment of that intent;

(2) terminate the existing state of emergency;

(3) immediately and unconditionally release Nelson Mandela and all others imprisoned and detained for their opposition to apartheid;

(4) establish political freedom and, specifically, lift the existing ban on the African National Congress and other political parties; and

(5) in the context of a suspension of violence on all sides, initiate a dialogue across lines of color, politics, and religion, with a view to establishing a nonracial and representative government.

These conditions emphasized the creation of a political atmosphere within South Africa that would allow viable negotiations. Thus discussions of sanctions led to the articulation of concrete, specific changes that could be interpreted as progress toward majority rule. The Commonwealth confirmed its role, first established in the Rhodesia settlement, of arbitrating the international legitimacy of the South African government.

21. These reports include the Commonwealth Committee of Foreign Ministers on Southern Africa, *South Africa: The Sanctions Report* (London: Penguin, 1989); Keith Ovenden and Tony Cole, *Apartheid and International Finance: A Program for Change* (London: Penguin, 1989); and Phyllis Johnson and David Martin, *Apartheid Terrorism: The Destabilization Report* (London: James Currey, 1989). All of these were prepared for the 1989 summit in Kuala Lumpur, Malaysia, where proponents of sanctions intended to argue for stricter financial sanctions. They were preempted by South Africa's successful negotiations with international creditors.

Legitimation and negotiation were also key issues in the establishment of the Eminent Persons Group (EPG), which the Commonwealth created in response to Britain's rejection of the initial package of economic sanctions. The Nassau meeting in 1985 established a group of "eminent persons" with a mandate to encourage the process of political dialogue and to investigate practical ways of promoting negotiations.[22] As a compromise between FLS demands for comprehensive mandatory sanctions and Britain's opposition to sanctions, the members set a trial period for the EPG, with a list of possible further sanctions to be enacted upon reevaluation six months later. These supplementary sanctions included bans on air links, new investment, agricultural imports, double taxation agreements, and tourist promotion, as well as on all government trade, procurement, and contracts. By the end of the summit meeting, members had thus agreed upon the establishment of the EPG, a list of partial sanctions (which, as noted above, included restrictions on new government loans, the import of Krugerrands, trade missions, computer sales, nuclear technology, oil, and arms), and this additional list of potential sanctions.

The EPG report filed six months later substantially bolstered proponents of sanctions. The group concluded that the South African government was not interested in negotiations. "It is our considered view," they wrote, "that, despite appearances and statements to the contrary, the South African Government is not yet ready to negotiate . . . except on its own terms. Those terms, both in regard to objectives and modalities, fall far short of reasonable black expectations and well-accepted democratic norms and principles."[23] The report also forcefully supported the inclusion of the African National Congress in any negotiations. The possible danger of South Africa to regional stability was underscored by South Africa's launching raids on neighboring countries precisely during its discussions with the EPG. The EPG's resulting pessimism about the potential for peaceful change in South Africa thus reinforced the emphasis by proponents of sanctions on the intransi-

22. The group comprised Malcolm Fraser, former Australian prime minister (nominated by Australia), co-chair; General Olusegun Obasango, former head of government of Nigeria (nominated by Zambia and Zimbabwe), co-chair; Lord Barber, chairman of Standard Chartered Bank and former British chancellor of the exchequer (nominated by Britain); Dame Nita Barrow, president of the World Council of Churches (Bahamas); John Malecela, former foreign minister of Tanzania (Zambia and Zimbabwe); Sardar Swaran Singh, former minister of external affairs in the Indian government (India); and Rev. Edward Walter Scott, primate of the Anglican Church of Canada (Canada).

23. Commonwealth Eminent Persons Group on Southern Africa, *Mission to South Africa: The Commonwealth Report* (London: Penguin, 1986), p. 131.

gence of the South African government and the need for substantial international action to end apartheid.

The EPG report led directly to the announcement by the Commonwealth of an additional package of sanctions, as had been established conditionally in the original guidelines from the Nassau summit. Britain, however, was still unwilling to abide by the group consensus and announced two of its own voluntary, less stringent sanctions—banning both new investment and promotion of tourism—in addition to declaring its intention to implement a possible European Economic Community ban on coal, iron, steel, and gold coins.[24] At a time when Canada and Australia increasingly supported the African position, the division between Britain and the rest of the Commonwealth was becoming entrenched. As a result, the mantle of leadership passed to Australia, Canada, and India.[25]

Thatcher explicitly broke the Commonwealth convention of consensus in 1987, when she (predictably) refused to join in further sanctions against South Africa.[26] This schism marked a fundamental change in the nature of the Commonwealth, with important ramifications for the South African issue in particular. Thatcher's willingness to defy the consensus severely limited the ability of other member states to use the Commonwealth as a forum for influencing British policy. Furthermore, Thatcher attempted throughout the latter half of the 1980s to shift the arena from the Commonwealth to Europe, as evident in her declared intention to abide by EEC decisions on sanctions. Clearly, Britain found more support for its position on South Africa within Europe,

24. Thatcher's agreement on even these minor measures was not a foregone conclusion; a number of states, such as Swaziland and Singapore, could possibly have sided with Britain. See Peter Lyon, "On from Nassau," *The Round Table* 297 (January 1986), p. 4. However, her agreement to even a few "measures" demonstrated that it was no longer possible to deny sanctions.

25. Peter Lyon, "The August Mini-Summit and After," *The Round Table* 300 (October 1986), p. 308. Ramphal also stresses the importance of the Australian and Canadian positions in avoiding a split along color lines; see "The Commonwealth since Saskatoon," *The Round Table* 301 (January 1987), p. 14.

26. At the 1985 meeting, for example, sanctions proponents hoped to convince Thatcher to join in a consensus sanctions package. By 1987 they focused more on establishing better monitoring and enforcement procedures for previously proclaimed measures, in part because they did not expect Thatcher to agree to further sanctions (*Globe and Mail*, 16 October 1987). Canada also proposed the creation of the Committee of Foreign Ministers as a compromise between African proponents of sanctions and Thatcher; Prime Minister Mulroney apparently had not anticipated the extent of African support and the active function created for that Committee (*Globe and Mail*, 19 October 1987).

with allies such as West Germany, than in the Third World–dominated Commonwealth.

Britain's discontent with the consensus among all the other members was even more apparent at the 1989 summit meeting in Kuala Lumpur, Malaysia. Thatcher took the unprecedented step of issuing a dissenting statement in reaction to the group's final communiqué. In her statement, she tried to demonstrate the "positive" approach to change in South Africa that her government was taking. She pointed to recent political reforms within South Africa as a sign of the need for "encouraging change rather than [furthering] punishment." She emphasized the negative aspects of sanctions, such as loss of jobs for blacks, and rejected the claim that sanctions have beneficial political effects.

In contrast, the consensus of the Commonwealth was that it was too early to judge definitively the significance of recent political changes in South Africa but that sanctions had indeed been increasingly beneficial in encouraging reform. Consequently, its members affirmed in Kuala Lumpur that sanctions should not be lifted without evidence of "clear and irreversible" change.[27] These diverging views of South Africa remained irreconcilable.

But regardless of Britain's distance from the prosanctions consensus, the Commonwealth established itself in the 1980s as an independent and significant factor in the evolving debates over anti-apartheid sanctions. Although commissioned as a compromise to circumvent Britain's dismissal of sanctions, the EPG report actually enhanced the prosanction position. It reinforced the growing predominance of the African regionalist perspective in the Commonwealth's assessments of southern Africa and fostered institutions, such as the Committee of Foreign Ministers, that further entrenched the perspective of the Frontline States. This consensus enhanced the Commonwealth's role in the processes of legitimation and negotiation, leading to increased international recognition of the liberation movements and of the incarcerated Nelson Mandela. In strong contrast to its significance in the early Commonwealth, Britain became weaker and more constrained than ever before.

Within the Commonwealth, as we have seen, the early debates over South Africa's membership established the constitutive principle of ra-

27. Thatcher's statement, "Southern Africa: The Way Ahead—Britain's View," is reprinted in *The Round Table* 313 (January 1990), 126–28, as is the official Commonwealth statement, "South Africa: The Way Ahead," and final communiqué, 97–102, 102–3. Debates like these persisted in reaction to political changes in South Africa in 1990.

cial equality. South Africa's preemptive withdrawal from the group shifted attention to Rhodesia as the other remaining bastion of white minority rule in southern Africa, but advocates of racial equality considered the two situations intimately related. Controversy over majority rule and sanctions against Rhodesia reduced Britain's dominance, as marked most notably by the establishment and growing strength of an independent Commonwealth secretariat. Furthermore, new collective actors, particularly the Frontline States, emerged as additional advocates of racial equality. Shifts in the responses of Dominion states to African pressures substantially increased the acceptance of anti-apartheid sanctions, despite Britain's continual objections. Acknowledging the inherent threat of apartheid to Commonwealth members, previous skeptics such as Australia and Canada decided to support both restrictions on South African trade and assistance to the neighboring Frontline States.

Although the African states did not achieve their full goal of comprehensive sanctions and British compliance, the evolution of Commonwealth policies offers an example of successful multilateral sanctions. Unlike those in the United Nations, sanctions advocates in the Commonwealth were not limited by procedural constraints such as veto powers, making mediation and consensus crucial for reaching agreements. As African experiences in the Commonwealth demonstrate, international institutions offer arenas for promoting norms and policy prescriptions, challenging the realist focus on hegemonic leadership. Refuting the neoliberal view of norms as constraints on behavior and demonstrating the constitutive implications of norm change, African (and broader Third World) advocacy of racial equality in the Commonwealth changed the fundamental character of the organization. This history highlights the importance of examining unconventional, loosely organized institutions, and it reinforces recent claims that multilateralism is a qualitatively distinct characteristic of certain international institutions.[28]

The case of Commonwealth sanctions, therefore, further undermines conventional sanctions analyses that rely on realist assumptions and deny the possibilities of cooperation. Commonwealth policies toward southern Africa demonstrate that legitimation should be considered a fundamental component of sanctions policies and collective action. By focusing on their consensus goal of a negotiated transition to a South African constitution based on universal suffrage, Commonwealth

28. See John Gerard Ruggie, "Multilateralism: The Anatomy of an Institution," *International Organization* 46 (Summer 1992), 561–98.

members also disproved the misleading realist presumption that the purpose of sanctions is to wage economic warfare. Selective economic measures (such as financial sanctions) that reflect an assessment of both the target country's global economic position, on the one hand, and explicit conditions for target response, on the other, are valuable practical lessons of the Commonwealth sanctions experience.

CHAPTER FIVE

The Organization
of African Unity

In both the United Nations and the Commonwealth, African states advocated sanctions against South Africa as part of a Pan-African perspective. As the regional response to apartheid in the Organization of African Unity demonstrates, a fundamental commitment to racial equality motivated African rejection of apartheid and provided a point of unity among states with diverse interests and perspectives. Realism's focus on structural security threats and national interests, however, offers little help in understanding how this regional consensus emerged and led to broader global activism; opposition to apartheid spanned Cold War divisions in the continent as a whole and among the Frontline States in particular. Nor does realism capture the African definition of security in terms of racial conflict and instability. African states allied against racism itself, and not simply in response to the balance of military capabilities and threats.[1]

Similarly, dependency theory's emphasis on structural economic interests, used more commonly than realism in analyzing African international relations, does not explain the patterns of African sanctions advocacy and opposition to apartheid. Especially for southern African states with substantial structural economic ties to South Africa, advocating sanctions risked both economic and military retaliation. Further-

---

1. South Africa's vastly superior military forces remained unchallenged. See Michael Evans, "The Security Threat from South Africa," in *Zimbabwe's Prospects,* ed. Colin Stoneman (London: Macmillan, 1988), pp. 218–35; Kent Hughs Butts and Paul R. Thomas, *Geopolitics in Southern Africa: South Africa as a Regional Superpower* (Boulder, Colo.: Westview Press, 1986).

73

*neoliberalism
& explain
costs*

more, contrary to neoliberal institutionalism's focus on the costs and benefits of cooperation, southern Africans bore substantial material costs for establishing alternative regional institutions rather than joining the low-cost—and economically advantageous—arrangements that the racist regional hegemon, South Africa, offered.[2]

Thus theories that predict that African states would simply respond to structural constraints or follow material incentives cannot explain their opposition to South Africa, which included costly regional economic restructuring and support for the anti-apartheid movement. The first section of this chapter traces these states' approach to the apartheid issue, from South Africa's initial exclusion through their support for liberation movements despite substantial incentives to compromise. In the second section I explore more recent regional cooperation, during which southern African states restructured their economic relations and military commitments in order to challenge South African hegemony in ways that both demonstrated the fundamental role of a commitment to racial equality and provided the framework for international intervention.

CONSTITUTIVE COMMITMENT TO RACIAL EQUALITY

During the era of decolonization in the 1960s, newly independent African states faced a plethora of choices in their foreign relations. Influential leaders advocated continental unity, although tensions arose over whether it should be in principle or form. Support for racial equality in southern Africa remained the one issue on which most states could agree, and debates at the end of the decade reaffirmed a continental commitment to that principle despite the potential economic benefits of cooperating with South Africa.

Pan-Africanism versus Sovereignty

Before decolonization, African international and regional politics revolved around the colonial powers. South Africa's foreign relations fo-

2. Neither class nor interest group analyses that rely on functional links among regional elites explain confrontation. Compare contributions in *Confrontation and Liberation in Southern Africa: Regional Directions after the Nkomati Accord*, ed. Ibrahim S. R. Msabaha and Timothy M. Shaw (Boulder, Colo.: Westview Press, 1987); Joseph Hanlon, *Beggar Your Neighbors: Apartheid Power in Southern Africa* (Bloomington: Indiana University Press, 1986); and Ronald T. Libby, *The Politics of Economic Power in Southern Africa* (Princeton: Princeton University Press, 1987).

cused on Britain and, to a lesser extent, Portugal (which controlled Mozambique and Angola until 1975). When most of the continent gained independence in the late 1950s and early 1960s, few of these new states inherited direct contacts with South Africa. One of their first foreign policy choices was whether to establish diplomatic, economic, and military ties with that country.

Most of the new African states advocated South Africa's isolation and called for the independence of British and Portuguese colonies in southern Africa. Consensus on decolonization and racial equality became a crucial unifying force among the various political factions in Africa. While personality clashes exacerbated disagreements on major issues such as continental unification, economic policies, and ties with former colonial powers, African leaders agreed that South Africa and the explicit racism of its apartheid policy signified a threat to Africa's overall peace and prosperity. Leaders of different political factions acknowledged that the welfare of Africans within South Africa and white minority–ruled territories in southern Africa was a legitimate concern for the continent as a whole, and that their liberation was a responsibility for all Africans.[3]

When African leaders met in Addis Ababa, Ethiopia, in May 1963 to negotiate the establishment of the Organization of African Unity, therefore, the major issue on which the three main factions could agree was racial equality in the context of decolonization.[4] The OAU Charter, however, also reaffirms state sovereignty and identifies threats of foreign intervention, reflecting concern over the Algerian war for independence and UN intervention in the Congo. Consequently, while the preamble evokes a determination to promote "a larger unity transcending ethnic and national differences," article 2 proclaims that the organization's purposes include promoting the unity and solidarity of the African states as well as defending their sovereignty and territorial integrity. Rather than establishing any supranational authority, the Assembly of Heads of State and Government, meeting on an annual basis,

3. Analysts generally identify three competing groups: the radical Casablanca group, associated with Nkrumah's vision of complete continental unity; the moderate Monrovia group, which envisioned more of a continental alliance; and a conservative francophone group, much less concerned with foreign intervention and neocolonialism. For details see Immanuel Wallerstein, *Africa: The Politics of Unity* (New York: Random House, 1967).

4. South Africa was not invited to participate in the OAU but, significantly, had been invited to the Conference of Independent African States that was held in Accra, Ghana in April 1958. South Africa declined to attend unless "responsible" (colonial) powers were included; this marked the last time South Africa was asked to attend any of the meetings that preceded the establishment of the OAU. See Wallerstein, *Africa*, p. 26.

became the main decision-making body, and even its decisions were not enforceable. The secretary-general of the OAU also remained weak. Informal rather than formal meetings and an emphasis on presenting a unified view to the outside world reinforced the OAU style of decision making by consensus.

Despite its voluntary nature, the group's fundamental consensus nevertheless had substantial implications for policies toward South Africa. Because South Africa's critics framed the issue of apartheid within the broader context of decolonization, opposition to apartheid within the OAU differed substantially from its forms within either the United Nations or the Commonwealth. The OAU never considered apartheid an issue of domestic jurisdiction, because South Africa was never a member. While South Africa was not specifically excluded from membership, its apartheid policies clearly contradicted the principles of the OAU Charter, the basis upon which states could seek membership. Since South Africa was never protected under the organization's stated norms of nonintervention and sovereignty, debate turned immediately to policy choices.

African calls for racial equality, support for liberation movements, and promotion of sanctions were recurring themes in the nascent OAU. However, tensions persisted over specific strategies. The member states supported sanctions in principle, as evident in the Charter's second agenda item (apartheid and racial discrimination), in which they announced their commitment to coordinating sanctions, pursuing the issue within the United Nations, and supporting South African refugees, in addition to condemning racial discrimination worldwide (with special attention drawn to the United States). In the mid-1960s, African opposition to Rhodesian independence reinforced the continental commitment to racial equality, but at the same time, independence for states neighboring South Africa highlighted the difficulties of carrying out the OAU's commitment to sanctions.[5]

Furthermore, the nature and extent of support for liberation in southern Africa became the focal point for numerous and evolving disagreements among member states. The strategic issue of confrontation versus compromise fueled these debates, which reached a crisis in the early 1970s. Sparking this controversy in 1969, the group's official Lusaka Manifesto emphasized negotiation and compromise, in contrast to the OAU's previous commitment to support for guerrilla move-

5. Sam C. Nolutshungu, *South Africa in Africa: A Study in Ideology and Foreign Policy* (New York: Africana, 1975), pp. 259–61.

76

ments. Because some members perceived the manifesto as signaling a retreat, especially in the face of concomitant South African initiatives toward continental detente under its "outward-looking policy," vociferous debate flared up over "dialogue" with the country.[6] With South Africa offering economic inducements to compromise, unified African opposition to white minority rule could no longer be taken for granted.

In November 1970, advocates of dialogue, led by Côte d'Ivoire, argued that armed struggle had failed, that African states were too weak militarily and economically to challenge South Africa, that a trade embargo was bound to fail, and, more constructively, that change among moderate whites could be encouraged through exchange.[7] In contrast, opponents stressed that the equality and dignity required for successful discussion and exchange were lacking and that the South African government should be negotiating with internal political movements rather than external states.

After protracted debate, the majority of OAU states at their June 1971 summit meeting in Addis Ababa rejected dialogue and reaffirmed the Lusaka Manifesto, which called for internal negotiation between the South African government and its own people. Furthermore, the majority criticized the minority member states for taking independent foreign policy positions on the issue, which in their view contradicted the charter.[8]

Members reaffirmed these positions in the Mogadishu Declaration of October 1971, which rejected South Africa's attempts at detente as an attempt to end its international isolation without abandoning apartheid. The OAU reaffirmed its "fullest support" to the armed struggle, promising to increase its "military, diplomatic, and moral" assistance. In

6. In adopting its new conciliatory policy, South Africa attempted to reduce its international isolation, especially with Third World countries in Asia and Latin America as well as Africa. See James Barber and John Barratt, *South Africa's Foreign Policy: The Search for Status and Security 1945–1988* (Cambridge: Cambridge University Press, 1990), chap. 8, and Nolutshungu, *South Africa in Africa*, chap. 7. All OAU documents are reprinted in *Africa Contemporary Record: Annual Survey and Documents*, ed. Colin Legum (New York: Africana, annual), and therefore will not be cited individually.

7. Zdenek Cervenka, *The Unfinished Quest for Unity: Africa and the OAU* (New York: Africana, 1977), p. 117; Nolutshungu, *South Africa in Africa*, pp. 269–78.

8. The minority were Côte d'Ivoire, Gabon, Lesotho, Malagasy, Malawi, and Mauritius. In addition, Benin, Niger, Swaziland, Togo, and Upper Volta abstained. Yet even those states advocating dialogue did not view this as accepting apartheid and held that Africa should act on apartheid within the OAU framework. See Cervenka, *Unfinished Quest*, p. 19; Nolutshungu, *South Africa in Africa*, pp. 276–77; Barber and Barratt, *South Africa's Foreign Policy*, p. 150.

77

addition to mentioning the possibility of sanctions against companies supporting South Africa, the declaration reiterated calls for NATO powers to cease military cooperation in colonial wars and for economic interests to cease supporting Portugal and South Africa. By 1972 "dialogue" was a dead issue, and even South Africa admitted a setback.[9] But disagreements among members persisted, particularly on implementing liberation support, leading to the devolution of authority to the Frontline States.

Liberation Support

Reaffirming their commitment to armed struggle, African states in the 1970s began developing a more specific strategy for their support. In 1963, OAU leaders had established an African Liberation Committee based in Tanzania. This committee became the vehicle for OAU financial assistance, through a special fund, and diplomatic recognition. Yet its lack of institutional authority over the liberation movements, inadequate financing, and continuing disagreements among African leaders limited the effectiveness of the Liberation Committee.[10] One remedy for these financial and logistical problems was to rank various liberation movements in order to concentrate resources. The Portuguese colonies, seen as most vulnerable, ranked first (receiving 70 percent of available resources), followed by Rhodesia, Namibia, and finally South Africa (whose opposition movements received only 5 percent of available resources).[11] After the Portuguese territories won independence in 1975, a sense of momentum and initiative intensified support for the Zimbabwean, Namibian, and South African liberation movements and strengthened the role of the emerging FLS informal alliance in implementing the OAU liberation strategy.[12]

9. Barber and Barratt, *South Africa's Foreign Policy*, p. 148.

10. Amadu Sesay, Olesola Ojo, and Orobola Fasehun, *The OAU after Twenty Years* (Boulder, Colo.: Westview Press, 1984), chap. 2; William J. Foltz and Jennifer Widner, "The OAU and Southern African Liberation," in *The OAU after Twenty Years*, ed. Yassin El-Ayouty and I. William Zartman (New York: Praeger, 1984).

11. Zdenek Cervenka, "The Tenth Anniversary of the OAU," in Legum, *Africa Contemporary Record, 1973–74*, p. A33.

12. On the origins of the FLS, see Carol B. Thompson, *Challenge to Imperialism: The Frontline States in the Liberation of Zimbabwe* (Boulder, Colo.: Westview Press, 1985); Robert Jaster, "A Regional Security Role for Africa's Frontline States," in *Southern Africa: Regional Security Problems and Prospects*, ed. Robert Jaster (London: Gower/IISS, 1985), pp. 88–132; and Gilbert M. Khadiagala, "The Front Line States in Southern African International Politics, 1975–1989" (Ph.D. diss., Johns Hopkins University, 1990).

Because their own leaders had succeeded in gaining independence through guerrilla war, Angola and Mozambique radicalized the faltering Liberation Committee (which they joined) and backed up those favoring a confrontational OAU strategy. While coalescing as an informal consultative group of states neighboring Rhodesia, the FLS soon operated as OAU agents with formal OAU endorsement (in April 1975 at the Dar es Salaam, Tanzania, summit) as an ad hoc committee of the Assembly of Heads of State and Government. Meeting in Quelimane, Mozambique, in February 1976, the FLS endorsed a confrontational strategy of supporting and unifying the various liberation groups. These states exercised more control over the liberation movements than had the OAU Committee primarily because they were sanctuary sites. As a result, they worked more effectively to unify and legitimize the various factions and rapidly gained international influence as recognized negotiators. The Frontline States' influence in the 1970s culminated in their crucial role in delivering a (temporarily) unified Zimbabwean liberation movement to the 1979 Lancaster House independence negotiations, and it continued in their intermediary role in Namibian negotiations.

While the Frontline States were establishing their legitimacy, both regionally and internationally, they further reinforced the OAU commitment to sanctions. Immediately after gaining its independence in 1975, Mozambique instituted sanctions against Rhodesia (as had Zambia in 1965), cutting its access to convenient ports and easy avenues for evading UN sanctions. Combined with its new role as a Zimbabwean guerrilla base, Mozambique's sanctions policy was crucial in the escalating regional military and economic pressure on the Rhodesian regime. Increasingly confrontational, the OAU as a whole also reendorsed regional and international sanctions, including measures against South Africa as well as Rhodesia, declaring at their 1975 meeting in Dar es Salaam that "Free Africa must maintain the economic, political, and cultural boycott" and "work for the total isolation of the South African regime."

Thus firmly established as a regional and international actor, the Frontline States added momentum for sanctions against South Africa by their collective opposition to white minority regimes and their support for the liberation movements. Dialogue and detente had been firmly rejected. The OAU reiterated its position that the only legitimate dialogue could be between the South African government and its opposition, the legitimate representatives of the South African people.

With Zimbabwe's independence in 1980, the FLS entered the next stage of opposing apartheid: restructuring regional relations.

Regional Cooperation

In the 1980s, two fundamental issues dominated regional debates in southern Africa: economic restructuring to decrease dependence on the South African economy and military cooperation to respond to South African destabilization policies. The Frontline States' response to these dual security issues reflected their Pan-Africanist view that apartheid caused economic exploitation and regional instability. Pan-African regionalism also framed broader international debates over the implementation of sanctions and other "positive measures," including military aid. Even when confronted with substantial economic and military costs, southern African states committed themselves to opposing apartheid and urged the great powers and international organizations to join them.

Economic Restructuring

Having implemented sanctions against Rhodesia, the Frontline States understood the importance of structural economic ties to South Africa, as well as the costs of breaking those ties. When Zimbabwe became an FLS member upon independence in 1980, the group addressed the structural weakness of the region's economy. Building on their security perspective of the 1970s, the group extended its informal cooperation under the auspices of the Southern African Development Coordination Conference, known as SADCC, their counter to South Africa's proposal of a "Constellation of Southern African States."[13]

The Frontline States used restructuring through SADCC to enhance regional diplomacy as well. Initially SADCC membership included three non-FLS members, Lesotho, Swaziland, and Malawi, and offered the prospect of membership to Namibia upon independence. Acknowledging their extreme vulnerability, the FLS did not pressure Lesotho or Swaziland to join their informal alliance. Malawi, in contrast, came un-

13. The Constellation concept also represented a shift in South African thinking toward developing ties with Africa in response to its own growing distrust of its traditional European economic partners as international criticism of apartheid escalated; Christopher R. Hill, "Regional Cooperation in Southern Africa," *African Affairs* 82 (April 1983), 217.

der more concerted pressure to join SADCC, in part as an attempt at conciliation after the harsh criticism its President Banda had received for supporting dialogue with South Africa. The Frontline States did limit their conciliatory efforts, however, by rejecting Zaire's interest in joining SADCC primarily because of its active support for rebel forces in Angola.[14]

While SADCC institutionalized regional economic cooperation, it explicitly acknowledged the security dimension—reducing dependence on South Africa—as its motivating force. At both the initial July 1979 meeting in Arusha, Tanzania, and the April 1980 Lusaka meeting, SADCC states declared their goals to be, first, reducing economic dependence, particularly (but not only) on South Africa; second, forging links to create a genuine and equitable regional integration; third, mobilizing resources to promote the implementation of national, interstate, and regional policies; and fourth, securing international cooperation within the framework of their strategy for economic liberation. Fragmentation, these leaders argued, would perpetuate exploitative colonial ties and lead to economic manipulation.[15]

Opposition to South Africa thus continued to serve as a unifying focus for African cooperation in the face of substantial political and economic differences. Indeed, the SADCC guidelines, which emphasized sectoral and productive cooperation rather than common-market liberalization of trading relations, made a regional economic strategy possible among a group of states with wide-ranging development ideologies and agendas. Mozambique, for example, stressed marxist centralization and state ownership, while Botswana emphasized foreign investment and freely convertible currency. Political variations were also great, with traditional monarchies, parliamentary systems, and one-party states. SADCC's unconventional strategy of minimal bureaucratic authority bridged these considerable political and economic differences.[16]

14. Khadiagala, "Front Line States in Southern African International Politics," chap. 5.

15. Frontline States, "Toward Economic Liberation," repr. in Legum, *Africa Contemporary Record 1979–80*, pp. C117–20; Southern African Development Coordination Conference, "Southern Africa: Toward Economic Liberation," repr. in *Africa Contemporary Record, 1980–81*, pp. C31–35. On these restructuring plans see *Southern Africa: Toward Economic Liberation*, ed. Amon J. Nsekela (London: Rex Collings, 1981), a collection of the initial sectoral papers.

16. On SADCC institutional structures, see Ismael Valigy and Helmut Dora, "The Creation of SADCC and the Problem of Transport," in *How Fast the Wind? Southern Africa, 1975–2000*, ed. Sergio Vieira, William G. Martin, and Immanuel Wallerstein (Trenton,

SADCC's motivations clearly linked economic security to anti-apartheid sanctions; member states seriously considered implementing their own sanctions and also examined the ramifications of broader Western measures. Well aware of the costs of sanctions after their Rhodesian experiences, southern African states could not entertain the idea of implementing economic sanctions without access to alternative trade and supply routes.[17] As a top priority, approximately 75 percent of the proposed projects targeted the transport and communication sector headed by Mozambique. SADCC particularly emphasized reestablishing the Beira Corridor route between Zimbabwe and Mozambique (previously cut as a sanction against Rhodesia) and improving the Tazara route connecting Zambia and Tanzania (established during Zambian sanctions against Rhodesia).[18] These alternative route would give SADCC states access to ports that were closer, supporters argued, offering substantial potential savings that justified the initial outlays.[19]

Despite the large investment needed for transportation restructuring, to the Frontline States and SADCC members persistent South African destabilization—the costs of apartheid—was intolerable. While the expenses of implementing their own sanctions and the repercussions of potential Western restrictions were undoubtedly high, the perpetuation of apartheid warranted immediate international and regional actions. SADCC's first comprehensive estimates of the damage from South African destabilization for the period 1980–84 totaled $10 billion, covering direct war destruction, extra defense expenditures, higher transport and energy expenses, smuggling, refugees, lost exports (including tourism), boycotts, loss of production, loss of eco-

N.J.: Africa World Press, 1992), pp. 133–63; for details on the various sectors, see *SADCC: Prospects for Disengagement and Development in Southern Africa*, ed. Samir Amin, Derrick Chitala, and Ibbo Mandaza (London: Zed Press/United Nations University, 1987).

17. Reginald H. Green, "The SADCC on the Front Line: Breakdown or Breakthrough?" in Legum, *Africa Contemporary Record 1986–87*, pp. A81–83. Note that southern African leaders—in contrast to many Western analysts—generally viewed sanctions against Rhodesia as successful. On the successful dimensions of Rhodesian sanctions, see William Minter and Elizabeth Schmidt, "When Sanctions Worked: The Case of Rhodesia Reexamined," *African Affairs* 87 (April 1988), 207–37.

18. In 1973, Mozambican ports handled one-fifth of South Africa's exports, two-thirds of Rhodesia's exports, one-half of Swaziland's exports, and all of Malawi's exports. Low levels of Portuguese investment during the last decade of its colonial rule exacerbated the cost of redeveloping Mozambican ports and railway connections. See Hanlon, *Beggar Your Neighbors*, pp. 131–32.

19. On these projects see Valigy and Dora, "Creation of SADCC."

nomic growth, and trading arrangements; others estimated the annual price of destabilization at $4 billion per year.[20]

SADCC members knew full well that substantial restructuring required significant external support; they thus sought international development aid. In the Arusha declaration, "Toward Economic Liberation," the Frontline States specifically called on governments, international institutions, and voluntary organizations to increase financial flows. Indeed, a number of their European-based and international advisors are often credited with developing and promoting the concept of a regional economic organization, and foreign money accounted for over 95 percent of the financing in most sectors.[21] Sweden and the other Nordic states collectively were the organization's largest donor.[22]

Support for SADCC became the institutional mechanism for international access to the region, as well as one route for international anti-apartheid work.[23] To enhance collective regional autonomy in economic decision making, SADCC stressed dialogue with external "cooperating partners" in an effort to create an atmosphere conducive to the exchange of ideas and criticisms. Through their efforts, claim its suppor-

---

20. The SADCC Report on the Costs of Destabilization is reprinted in Hanlon, *Beggar Your Neighbors*, pp. 265–70. See also Reginald H. Green and Carol B. Thompson, "Political Economies in Conflict: SADCC, South Africa, and Sanctions," in *Destructive Engagement: Southern Africa at War*, ed. David Martin and Phyllis Johnson (Harare: Zimbabwe Publishing House, 1986), pp. 245–80. Evaluations of these costs remained contentious. Joseph Hanlon even argued that SADCC states would benefit from international sanctions; see "On the Front Line: Destabilization, the SADCC States, and Sanctions," in *Sanctions against Apartheid*, ed. Mark Orkin (Cape Town: David Philip, 1990), pp. 173–88, and "Impact of Sanctions on SADCC," in *South Africa: The Sanctions Report, Documents, and Statistics*, ed. Joseph Hanlon (London: James Currey, 1990), pp. 293–304. In strong contrast, Lloyd John Chingambo and Stephen Chan argued that substantial vulnerabilities and potential costs were too frequently overlooked; see "Sanctions and South Africa: Strategies, Strangleholds, and Self-Consciousness," *Paradigms* 2 (Winter 1988–89), pp. 112–32.

21. Hill, "Regional Cooperation," p. 224. For a breakdown of projects and extent of international financial participation, see Valigy and Dora, "Creation of SADCC."

22. See David R. Black, "Australian, Canadian, and Swedish Policies toward Southern Africa: A Comparative Study of Middle Power Internationalism" (Ph.D. diss., Dalhousie University, 1992), chap. 8.

23. Not all analysts, however, have been optimistic about the consequences of such external involvement, warning of international dependency replacing regional dependency. See Roger Leys and Arne Tostensen, "Regional Cooperation in Southern Africa: The Southern African Development Coordination Conference," *Review of African Political Economy* 23, (January–April 1982), 52–71; Amin, Chitwala, and Mandaza, *SADCC;* and Gilbert M. Khadiagala, "The Front Line States, Regional Interstate Relations, and Institution Building in Southern Africa," in *Toward Peace and Security in Southern Africa*, ed. Harvey Glickman (New York: Gordon and Breach, 1990), pp. 131–61.

ters, SADCC achieved an international image of competence and credibility, and developed the unusual ability to be innovative while avoiding manipulation by donors.[24] But despite these optimistic claims of its supporters, certainly not all donors were equally willing to abide by its agendas and initiatives. A number of Western countries saw SADCC as a potential means for tempering the radicalism of marxist Angola and Mozambique and promoting capitalism in the region. West Germany resisted working through SADCC-determined priorities, but it eventually moderated its resistance. Both Britain under Thatcher and the United States under Reagan held similar views. Other conservative European countries attempted to channel their support to projects that would not decrease regional economic links to South Africa. Even the more liberal European states saw cooperation with SADCC as a way of enhancing their access to resources and markets in the region.[25]

Soliciting international support, especially for transportation sector projects, became more important in 1986, when SADCC states (notably Commonwealth members) began serious discussions of implementing their own economic sanctions against South Africa. The Frontline States were particularly eager to refute the argument that concern for blacks in the region, and within South Africa itself, precluded implementing sanctions. In contrast, South Africa, as well as conservatives in Britain and the United States, had developed a sudden concern for the welfare of blacks.[26] Nevertheless, SADCC endeavored to direct these conservatives' declared wishes for the welfare of the region into support for its transportation projects.

The Frontline States' emphasis on developing alternative transportation routes, such as the Beira Corridor, further illustrates the connec-

24. Reginald H. Green, "SADCC in 1985: Economic Regionalism in a War Zone," in Legum, *Africa Contemporary Record 1985–86*, pp. A107–8; while frequently reporting on SADCC, Green has also been an advisor to SADCC.

25. Hanlon, *Beggar Your Neighbors*, pp. 25–26. In contrast, Sweden (and the Nordic countries) are noteworthy for aid policies that responded to, rather than placed conditions on, southern African states' initiatives; a substantial amount of their aid went to SADCC transportation and communications projects, notably Beira and Tazara. Sweden also gave substantial aid to the more radical states of Angola and Mozambique while avoiding support for Malawi and Swaziland, which had received South African assistance. See Black, "Australian, Canadian, and Swedish Policies."

26. On the insufficiency of FLS contingency plans, see Douglas Anglin, "The Frontline States and Sanctions against South Africa," in *Sanctioning Apartheid*, ed. Robert E. Edgar (Trenton, N.J.: Africa World Press, 1990), pp. 255–92; and Chingambo and Chan, "Sanctions and South Africa." On these conservative positions, see chaps. 6 and 7 below, as well as Joseph Hanlon and Roger Omond, *The Sanctions Handbook* (London: Penguin, 1987).

tions between regional economic and military security for southern African decision makers. While leaders at times defended economic restructuring on its own terms, the broad differences in economic orientation among its member states demonstrated that SADCC was founded more in response to the shared threat from South Africa than as a source of a coherent economic plan. Indeed, South Africa's responses to SADCC—notably in the form of military attacks on Mozambican transport routes through proxies—only strengthened regional FLS cooperation.

Strategic Alliance

The threat from destabilization provided a common framework for regional policy. Economic stability, regime security, and military protection were inseparable for all the states in the area. Mozambique—and joint defense of its government—became the focal point for responding to South Africa.

Having served as a military base for Zimbabwean guerrillas and implemented sanctions during the Rhodesian war, Mozambique early on became South Africa's target. After Zimbabwe's independence in 1980, the formerly Rhodesian-controlled Mozambique National Resistance (known as Renamo) came under South African oversight, and the group shifted their reliance for weapons supplies to South Africa.[27] South Africa perceived the Mozambican government as the cornerstone of regional opposition, as a crucial supporter of ANC guerrillas infiltrating across their common border, and also as an extension of Soviet control in Africa.

By 1984 the combination of prior sanctions against Rhodesia and the economic and political dislocations due to continual Renamo activity in the countryside had substantially weakened Mozambique. In addition, its appeals to the Eastern Bloc for military support had failed; indeed, the Soviets urged Mozambique to seek an accommodation with South Africa rather than military confrontation.[28] The West's similar advice, which Mozamibique's President Machel received during his

27. For details of Renamo activities and South African support, see Allen Isaacman, "Mozambique," *Survival* (January–February 1988), 14–38; Phyllis Johnson and David Martin, *Apartheid Terrorism: The Destabilization Report* (London: James Currey, 1989), chap. 1; and Alex Vines, *Renamo: Terrorism in Mozambique* (London: James Currey, 1991).

28. Colin Legum, "The Nkomati Accord and Its Implications for the Front Line States and South Africa," in *Confrontation and Liberation in Southern Africa: Regional Directions after the Nkomati Accord*, ed. Ibrahim S. R. Msabaha and Timothy M. Shaw (Boulder, Colo.: Westview Press, 1987), pp. 92–94; Isaacman, "Mozambique," p. 25.

tour of European capitals in October 1983, was less surprising. Faced with the serious possibility of losing power, Machel conceded to a security treaty with South Africa, the Nkomati Accord, signed at their border in March 1984. Upon announcing the "agreement on nonaggression and good neighborliness," Mozambique expelled ANC representatives in exchange for South Africa's pledge to end support for Renamo.

The Nkomati Accord sent shock waves through the region. While some Frontline States initially criticized Machel, their concern for the survival of his government moderated their public response. In addition to their skepticism about South Africa's intentions to abide by the agreement, neighboring states also feared that Mozambique's capitulation would lead South Africa to increase its covert activities, in order to coerce further security accords and erode the ANC's regional base. South Africa's attempts to expand upon Nkomati diplomatically were unsuccessful, however, in part because of growing evidence of its continuing support to Renamo.

As it became clear that South Africa was still supplying Renamo, the Frontline commitment to Mozambican security grew; Mozambique officially suspended the accord in October 1985, after acquiring concrete proof of South African noncompliance. While Mozambique pledged to continue its war against Renamo, the FLS resolved to support Mozambique at a meeting between Tanzania's Nyerere, Zimbabwe's Mugabe, and Machel in Harare, Zimbabwe, in June 1985.[29] Zimbabwean military involvement in Mozambique escalated in 1985–86, particularly along the Beira Corridor, and Frontline leaders increased pressures for a regional military commitment to resist South African destabilization efforts. Their focus was Malawi.

Malawi had made itself infamous in the past by supporting dialogue with South Africa, establishing diplomatic relations with South Africa, and, more recently, accepting its economic assistance. With Malawi's general commitment to liberation under considerable doubt, Renamo incursions across the Malawian-Mozambican border in mid-1986 led many observers and leaders to conclude that President Banda supported Renamo and that South Africa's diplomatic presence in the country offered it logistical advantages as well.[30] Renamo had no known permanent camps in Malawi, but eyewitness reports claimed that its

29. Khadiagala, "Front Line States, Regional Interstate Relations," p. 138.
30. *Africa Research Bulletin* 23 (15 August 1986), 8156; Isaacman, "Mozambique," p. 26.

forces were crossing back and forth across the border, and Malawi had made no attempts to curb South African aircraft from dropping supplies. Whatever the reasons for Banda's tolerance of South African destabilization, the refugee problem created undeniable economic and political difficulties for the Malawian government.[31]

For the Frontline States, however, Malawi's support for (or tolerance of) Mozambican destabilization was unconscionable. Their pressures on Banda escalated on 11 September 1986 to a warning by Zambia's Kaunda, Mugabe, and Machel that they were prepared to block the export routes of landlocked Malawi. Banda, however, denied assisting Renamo, although he admitted that attacks may have happened without his government's knowledge or approval. Machel threatened closing and arming the common borders. Mugabe and Kaunda stressed their intention of implementing sanctions against South Africa, including shutting down borders to South African goods, a measure that would hurt Malawi and Zaire.[32] After the threat of blockade, Banda expelled Renamo forces in October 1986.

Tensions between the Frontline States and Malawi remained high, however, in the aftermath of Machel's death in October. While South Africa was accused of causing the mysterious plane accident that killed the Mozambican leader, demonstrators focused on Malawian embassies, primarily in Mozambique but also in Zimbabwe. Furthermore, South African foreign minister Pik Botha made allegations that Machel and Mugabe had been plotting Banda's overthrow, based on apparent evidence found on Machel's plane (which had crashed in South African territory). The Zimbabwean and Mozambican governments dismissed Botha's charges as having been fabricated in a blatant attempt at divisiveness.[33]

After October, however, Malawi increasingly cooperated with the attempts of the Frontline States to establish a regional security arrangement in response to destabilization. The December 1986 Lilongwe Agreement established a joint security commission with Mozambique; Malawi also granted permission to Mozambique and Zimbabwe for mil-

---

31. *Africa Confidential* 27 (3 September 1986), 5; Isaacman, "Mozambique," p. 27. While most analysts view Banda as having had monolithic control over Malawian policy, both Hanlon, *Beggar Your Neighbors,* and Libby, *Politics of Economic Power,* stress the role of domestic divisions and power struggles in Malawi's regional policies.

32. *Africa Research Bulletin* 23 (15 October 1986), 8218-89.

33. Pik Botha claimed to possess incomplete minutes from a meeting between Machel and Zimbabwean intelligence chief Emmerson Mnangagwa; *Africa Research Bulletin* 23 (15 December 1986), 8291-92.

itary operations against rebels in its territory.[34] Tanzania also increased the number of its troops in northern Mozambique to counter an increased Renamo presence, primarily of guerrillas ejected from Malawi, and to defend the Ncala rail line. The new Mozambican leader, Joaquim Chissano, had asked for full Tanzanian military intervention (along the lines of the Tanzanian invasion of Uganda in 1979 to oust Idi Amin); as a compromise, President Mwinyi sent three thousand troops in November 1986 and an additional two thousand troops in February 1987. By April 1987 Malawi had also sent three hundred troops into northern Mozambique to defend the Ncala line. Although the number of troops represented a token measure, their deployment signaled a Malawian shift away from South Africa toward the FLS.[35]

The FLS regional commitment to Mozambican security was also instrumental in obtaining additional international military assistance. For example, beginning in late 1986 Britain offered military training to the Mozambican army, and by 1987 the Commonwealth included military support as part of their regional policy. Other Western governments, including Italy, France, and Portugal, also improved their security relationships with Mozambique, while Renamo proved unable to garner substantial international support, even from the Reagan administration in the United States.[36] Development aid supporters also increasingly viewed the region in terms of interconnected economic and military security dimensions, as illustrated in SADCC's January 1988 summit in Arusha, where members explicitly considered the military-security dimension of its economic projects; donors increasingly viewed military assistance as a necessary safeguard for development projects.

The late 1980s marked the height of international responses to the Pan-African perspective on regional security. Yet just as the West began to acknowledge the connections between economic and military security for the southern African states, South African destabilization eased.

34. Khadiagala, "Front Line States in Southern African International Politics," p. 29; Isaacman, "Mozambique," p. 31.

35. Khadiagala, "Front Line States, Regional Interstate Relations," p. 145; Isaacman, "Mozambique," p. 31. The FLS also discussed a Nigerian offer of assistance, which was vetoed by Zimbabwe. Despite this increase in regional military cooperation, suggestions for a more formalized African Defense Force (a recurring but minor theme since the OAU's founding) continued to be rejected. On the arguments for and against, see Michael Evans, "The Frontline States, South Africa, and Southern African Security: Military Prospects and Perspectives" (Harare: University of Zimbabwe Press, 1986), and Hasu Patel, "Zimbabwe," *Survival*, (January–February 1988), 55–56.

36. Isaacman, "Mozambique," p. 33. However, Chingambo and Chan, "Sanctions and South Africa," stress the inadequacy of this military aid.

After its defeat at Cuito Cuanavale in Angola in 1988, South Africa revised its regional strategy.[37] By September 1988, South Africa and Mozambique had renewed talks and revived joint monitoring under the Nkomati Accord (although evidence indicates that, once again, South Africa did not completely suspend its support to Renamo), while Portugal, Zimbabwe, and Tanzania jointly attempted to mediate a truce between the Mozambican government and Renamo. South Africa's own military strength had been weakened, in part by the international arms embargo, and international criticism of its regional policies had escalated. By 1989, with Namibian independence and F. W. de Klerk's election in South Africa, the conditions for regional conciliation had much improved.

African activism was an essential component of the international anti-apartheid movement. In addition to advocating sanctions in the United Nations and Commonwealth, the OAU's support for liberation movements furthered decolonization in southern Africa and increased pressure for the elimination of apartheid in South Africa. While the Frontline States sustained considerable economic and military costs for their opposition to South Africa, they successfully encouraged international support for the global sanctions movement, regional economic restructuring, and security aid to Mozambique. They had not intended to provoke a cycle of retaliation, but the South African response indeed convinced the world of the primary tenet of the Pan-Africanist strategy: that apartheid created regional instability.

African consensus, even on the issue of racial equality, should not be taken for granted. These states faced numerous incentives to recognize South Africa, as well as retaliatory threats for advocating sanctions. Sanctions advocates, in other words, absorbed considerable direct and opportunity costs for the intangible benefits of supporting a constitutive norm of racial equality. Yet conventional sanctions analysts, focusing on continuing trade relations in southern Africa, miss both the role of the African states in promoting global sanctions and the considerable costs that the Frontline States incurred in trying to restructure economic relations. Thus the actions of southern African states follow neither conventional alliance perspectives nor liberal market perspectives.

The OAU and FLS responses to apartheid confirm a more general

37. See Robert Davies, "After Cuito Cuanavale: The New Regional Conjuncture and the Sanctions Question," in Orkin, *Sanctions against Apartheid,* pp. 198–206.

critique that realist analysis of sanctions focuses exclusively on coercive power and the behavioral response of target states.[38] Sanctions analyses, too, should recognize the importance of economic structures and the role of norms in defining threats. Without a Pan-African commitment to racial equality, there would have been no international anti-apartheid sanctions movement.

38. David A. Baldwin, *Economic Statecraft* (Princeton: Princeton University Press, 1985).

PART III

BILATERAL POLICIES

CHAPTER SIX

The United States

Conventional theories of international relations emphasize the role of hegemons in initiating multilateral policies and underwriting the costs of cooperation. Yet these theories cannot explain U.S. sanctions against South Africa, particularly during a peak period of concern over Soviet challenge. Structural theories that acknowledge solely strategic or economic interests predict strong U.S. ties in the postwar era but not the adoption of sanctions.[1] Following on these materialist assumptions, conventional sanctions analyses cannot clarify why the United States followed rather than led in adopting sanctions. Even regime theories that recognize international norms cannot elucidate why the United States responded to rather than initiated, global pressures for racial equality. Indeed, the United States consistently vetoed UN resolutions calling for mandatory economic sanctions; regime constraint remained weak.

Since it was congressional action in opposition to Reagan administration policy that succeeded in establishing U.S. sanctions, analysts frequently conclude that domestic political considerations account for the

1. Those concerned about U.S. strategic interests emphasized crucial mineral deposits and vulnerable sea-lanes; many also pointed to the importance of maintaining a market economy in South Africa to counter the spread of communism. In addition, U.S.-based multinational corporations had significant interests in the South African economy. On U.S. interests in the region, see William Minter, *King Solomon's Mines Revisited: Western Interests and the Burdened History of Southern Africa* (New York: Basic Books, 1986); Study Commission on U.S. Policy toward Southern Africa, *South Africa: Time Running Out* (Berkeley, Cal.: University of California Press, 1981); Christopher Coker, *The United States and South Africa 1968–1985: Constructive Engagement and Its Critics* (Durham, N.C.: Duke University Press, 1986).

policy change.[2] Indeed, this argument follows conventional levels of analysis, as both structural realism and regimes theories suggest. However, considering U.S. domestic politics in isolation from their international context neglects a crucial transnational dimension of these pressures to support of racial equality. Anti-apartheid activists, initially Pan-Africanists and later a broadly based coalition of domestic groups, promoted congressional sanctions in concert with the global anti-apartheid movement. Considered alone, an explanation based on domestic politics leaves open a number of questions, including why policy toward South Africa became a salient domestic issue and why U.S. sanctions coincided with a global response to apartheid.

The extraordinary success of transnational anti-apartheid activists in generating U.S. sanctions against South Africa offers evidence that norms, independent of strategic and economic considerations, are an important factor in determining great powers' policies. In the first section of this chapter, I explore the transnational origins of domestic U.S. demands for sanctions. In the second, I examine the debates over sanctions in the mid-1980s. What is most remarkable about domestic demands for racial equality and sanctions is that previously marginal arguments for democracy became a fundamental component of the definition of U.S. interests.

MOBILIZING DEMANDS FOR RACIAL EQUALITY

The unprecedented success of the transnational anti-apartheid movement in mobilizing support for sanctions was predicated on uniting concern over the two issues of domestic race relations and South African apartheid. Activists achieved this goal by both framing the apartheid issue in the context of the prevailing civil rights discourse of equality and increasing their institutional access to decision-making power. By the 1980s, their argument that racial equality could no longer simply be ignored or sacrificed to preserve stability and profits in southern Africa had gained national salience.

2. Case study analyses of policy during the Reagan years focus on the relationship between Congress and the executive but frequently differ on who should get the credit (or blame) for policy change. Compare, e.g., Pauline Baker, *The United States and South Africa: The Reagan Years* (New York: Ford Foundation, 1989), and the autobiography of the assistant secretary of state for African affairs, Chester Crocker, *High Noon in Southern Africa: Making Peace in a Rough Neighborhood* (New York: Norton, 1992).

Transnational Origins of Anti-Apartheid Pressures

African-American attention to Africa, and to South Africa in particular, is neither novel nor surprising. For adherents of Pan-Africanism—historically the core of African-American activism on African issues—racial discrimination in South Africa and the United States were logically connected through the view that "black emancipation [is] a necessary state for the full development of blacks everywhere."[3] Reaching as far back as the transatlantic slave trade to develop political awareness, early Pan-Africanist leaders such as Marcus Garvey were active in the "Back to Africa" movement of the 1920s. Often referred to as the "father of Pan-Africanism," W. E. B. Du Bois cofounded the National Association for the Advancement of Colored People (NAACP). Pan-Africanist ideology also strongly influenced African independence leaders, many of whom were educated in the United States, and it shaped their views of South African apartheid. In turn, those African leaders influenced many African-American activists.[4] Sharing a common intellectual heritage, African and African-American political leaders maintained and enhanced their personal ties.

During the McCarthy era, however, African-American organizations such as the Council on African Affairs were subjected to Justice Department investigation following accusations of subversive activities.[5] Consequently, African-Americans focused more on civil rights issues at home, while liberal whites, a constituency of activists, scholars, business elites,

3. Bernard Makhosezwe Magubane, *The Ties That Bind: African-American Consciousness of Africa* (Trenton, N.J.: Africa World Press, 1987), p. 230. Also, the 1963 charter of the OAU drew attention to issues of racial equality in the United States; see chap. 5 above.

4. Magubane emphasizes the persistent comparisons between the American and South African situations; he cites in particular four Nobel Peace Prize winners: African-Americans Dr. Ralph Bunche and Dr. Martin Luther King, Jr., and South Africans Chief Albert Luthuli and Rev. Bishop Desmond Tutu (*Ties That Bind*, p. 230).

5. The Council on African Affairs, run by radicals Max Yergen and Paul Robeson, disbanded in 1955 after growing government harassment. Transnational Pan-African connections were purposely downplayed in the 1950s in favor of a focus on civil rights, because African-Americans feared being portrayed as communists. The history of the council—including disagreements between Yergen and Robeson over its orientation—indicates a more fundamental tension between Pan-African and communist thinking. Advocating a more radical stance, Robeson won control of the council in 1948. See Philip V. White, "The Black American Constituency for Southern Africa, 1940–1980," in *The American People and South Africa: Publics, Elites, and Policymaking Processes*, ed. Alfred O. Hero, Jr. and John Barratt (Lexington, Mass.: Lexington Books, 1981), pp. 83–102, and Hollis R. Lynch, *Black American Radicals and the Liberation of Africa: The Council on African Affairs 1937–1955* (Ithaca: Cornell University Africana Studies and Research Center, 1978).

and church leaders who generally were isolated from the black community, dominated policy toward Africa through the proliferation of organizations such as the African-American Institute, the American Committee on Africa, and the African Studies Association.[6]

Decolonization in the 1960s revived African-American interest in African affairs; many of the new African heads of state, notably Kwame Nkrumah of Ghana, were themselves ardent advocates of Pan-Africanism. The Sharpeville killings in South Africa in 1960 also drew African-American attention to the southern part of the continent. As early as 1962, civil rights spokesman Dr. Martin Luther King, Jr., and South African chief Albert Luthuli (then president of the African National Congress) issued a joint statement calling for the imposition of international sanctions against South Africa.[7] Organization improved.

Emerging out of the American Society of African Culture (which had been the main black representative group of the 1950s), the American Negro Leadership Conference on Africa convened in 1962 with representatives from major African-American civil rights groups and unions. At its second meeting in 1964, the group called for stronger U.S. policies against white South Africa, including prohibition on future investments and support for UN arms, oil, and economic sanctions. Closer to home, the conference called for lobbying efforts in Washington, legal aid for victims of apartheid, and additional educational endeavors. Furthermore, the participants explicitly linked civil rights, the international image of the U.S., and its interests in Africa. However, the group faltered soon after its third meeting in 1967 because of its failure to mobilize domestic support for its program.[8]

Through the more race-conscious civil rights and Black Power movements of the 1960s, African-Americans articulated a stronger vision of transnational interests in African affairs, one reminiscent of the earlier Pan-Africanism of Du Bois and Garvey.[9] Malcolm X founded the Organization of Afro-American Unity (patterned on the Organization of African Unity), while other leaders advocated solidarity with oppressed peoples of the Third World generally and blacks in South Africa specifically. As their own movements radicalized, African-Americans' interest

6. See Martin Staniland, *American Intellectuals and African Nationalists, 1955–1970* (New Haven: Yale University Press, 1991).

7. Magubane, *Ties That Bind*, p. 216.

8. White, "Black American Constituency," p. 87.

9. Locksley Edmondson, "Black America as a Mobilizing Diaspora: Some International Implications," in *Modern Diasporas in International Politics*, ed. Gabriel Shaffer (New York: St. Martin's, 1986), pp. 183–85.

focused increasingly on liberation movements, primarily those in the southern African region that had launched military actions against colonial and apartheid rule.

By the end of the 1960s, African-American activists and politicians had committed themselves to pursuing their interest in African affairs. Representative Charles Diggs, a founding member of the Congressional Black Caucus (CBC), assumed the chair of the House Foreign Affairs Subcommittee on Africa in 1969. In a less institutionalized setting, two African-American workers started a protest movement against the Polaroid Corporation, demanding the end of sales of photographic equipment that the South African government used to enforce its controversial pass-law system, which restricted blacks' travel, employment, and housing.[10]

In reaction to the arguments over the responsibilities of corporations such as Polaroid, the Reverend Leon Sullivan, himself an African-American corporate board member, devised the so-called Sullivan Principles: guidelines for corporate strategies to enhance the living and working conditions of black South Africans. Criticizing these principles and the philosophy behind them, advocates of divestment, on the other hand, saw such ameliorative measures as drastically insufficient; they argued for both complete corporate withdrawal and governmental (and international) enforcement of economic disengagement.

Two dimensions of anti-apartheid debate thus emerged out of the Polaroid controversy: corporate responsibility and U.S. government policy. Both institutionalized and grassroots protests spread throughout the 1970s, with significant repercussions. Debates over apartheid had begun to reach the national level.

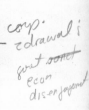

Apartheid as a National Issue

Political pressure for sanctions had grown substantially more organized and visible by the late 1970s. Following the Black Leadership Conference on Southern Africa (held in September 1976 in Gary, Indi-

10. In response to protests, Polaroid stopped sales of products used in the pass system. The workers' movement, however, considered this inadequate and, while picketing headquarters, demanded a boycott of Polaroid products. The company sent a fact-finding mission to South Africa, which returned recommending better benefits for black South African workers (salaries, training, educational opportunities) within the context of the benefits of an expanding economy. Well publicized, Polaroid's position foreshadowed the antidivestment position of most corporations during the subsequent debates of the 1970s and 1980s. On the Polaroid controversy, see White, "Black American Constituency," pp. 89–90.

ana), groups under the aegis of the CBC and the NAACP established TransAfrica (in 1977) with a mandate to lobby the government on African and Caribbean issues. Under the leadership of Randall Robinson (former assistant to Representative Diggs), the organization garnered support from elected officials, specialists on Africa, religious leaders, and other observers of African affairs in its efforts to force action on the South Africa issue.[11] Not surprisingly, the House Subcommittee on Africa was the prime target of their pressure (during the Carter presidency Robinson also had direct access to important State Department and administration figures).[12]

In addition to continuing activists' protest and direct influence on the executive branch, TransAfrica's cooperation with the CBC signified a shift toward electoral politics. The alliance marked the incorporation of Pan-Africanist internationalism into the more politically mainstream integrationist perspective, linking domestic issues of black freedom to African ones. Advocates of sanctions argued that U.S. interests were best served by allying with the black South African majority.[13] While the discourse and targets of protest widened, the societal base for activism also expanded.

In response to the dramatically escalating conflict within South Africa in 1984, TransAfrica spearheaded public protest about apartheid when its director and a small group of activists began taking their complaints directly to the South African embassy in Washington, D.C. Quickly arrested and then released, these protesters, under the mantle of their newly formed "Free South Africa" movement, coordinated a continuous flow of pickets outside the embassy in the ensuing months. National visibility rose as demonstrations began to include prominent personalities (for example, music star Stevie Wonder and former presi-

11. On Robinson and TransAfrica, see Henry F. Jackson, *From Congo to Soweto: U.S. Foreign Policy toward Africa since 1960* (New York: William Morrow, 1982), pp. 123–26. Initially, in the late 1970s, TransAfrica lobbying focused on the issue of Rhodesia, although white minority rule in both was seen as one inseparable issue.

12. During the 1976 presidential campaign, Jimmy Carter spoke of the need to increase the role of African-Americans in foreign policy including toward Africa. The subsequent important role of Carter's appointment of civil rights activist Andrew Young as permanent representative to the United Nations did not forestall continued pressure from both African-Americans and other activists for a stronger U.S. response to South African racial policies, but it did blur the previous distinction between external pressure on government policy and participation in policy making itself. African leaders as well as African-Americans were disappointed in Young's lack of support for sanctions. See Jackson, *Congo to Soweto*, pp. 153–60.

13. On TransAfrica's position, see Randall Robinson, "The Reagan Administration and South Africa," *TransAfrica Forum* 1 (Summer 1982), 3–6.

dent Carter's daughter, Amy) as well as members of Congress (including Republican senator Lowell Weicker of Connecticut). Sympathizers across the country began similar protests at other South African consulate facilities.

Allied grassroots groups throughout the country helped disperse pressure from the federal level to corporations, state and local governments, and investment groups (including universities, pension funds, and other private investors). As one TransAfrica activist explained, this broad-based coalition was "no more a civil rights movement than it is a labor movement or a religious movement or a celebrities movement, though people from all of those categories of our population have given of their substance, and sometimes have offered their bodies, to support this endeavor."[14] These various groups had histories of protesting for divestment, but they were no longer acting on their own. Protests became more coordinated and began to receive greater publicity.

The divestment movement gained strength as it shifted to a similar strategy of protests at corporation headquarters. Escalating involvement in the "corporate campaign" engulfed diverse grassroots movements, including those based in universities and church groups. These activists hoped to provoke divestment by shareholders or disinvestment by corporations with South African operations; in addition, public education about the nature of apartheid fueled public demand for some type of policy response to the escalating violence within South Africa itself.[15] U.S. governmental response to South Africa was now the center of political conflict.

Advocacy of sanctions and divestment had become part of a political perspective that identified implicit and explicit support for white minority rule, by both American corporations and the U.S. government, as detrimental to the process of political reform within South Africa. Put succinctly, proponents of this view argued that "Americans are getting rich from the semi-slave labor of black South Africans and our government is encouraging them to continue doing that."[16] Activists

14. Roger Wilkins, "Demonstrating Our Opposition," *Africa Report* 30 (May–June 1985), 30.
15. Wilkins, an organizer of the "Free South Africa" movement, claimed that the timing of the protests to follow upon President Reagan's reelection in November 1984 was coincidental; he said the demonstrations were inspired by the South African government's adoption of its new constitution and the concomitant escalation in political repression and violent conflict. The protests, he claimed, were aimed at increasing awareness of South African repression (ibid.).
16. Ibid., p. 31.

advocated a twofold response: corporate economic withdrawal and restrictions on relations with the South African government. The prosanctions policy perspective had never before been articulated to the
highest-ranking policy makers.

Numerous voices within both society and government contributed to
linking apartheid to more pervasive support of (or at least tolerance of)
racism. In 1984, the Reverend Jesse Jackson, a longtime African-American civil rights activist, brought the issue of apartheid into his presidential campaign, provoking his more centrist opponents to address the
topic in their pronouncements.[17] To gain national attention, clearly this
linkage had to be articulated in terms that appealed to more mainstream politicians than had the prior Pan-Africanist conceptualizations,
which appealed to African-Americans and left-oriented activists. National politicians, with a few notable exceptions, had become aware of
the potentially damaging connection between the perception of support for apartheid and tolerance of racism at home.[18]

Whereas only a few members of Congress, other than those of the
CBC, had previously given much attention to African issues, numerous
high-ranking senators and representatives seized upon the apartheid
issue in late 1984. The context of U.S. race relations became crucial in
shaping the direction of policy toward South Africa. Anti-apartheid
protesters had fundamentally altered the terms of public—and congressional—debate over policy toward South Africa.

REDEFINING NATIONAL INTERESTS

The political salience of the arguments of sanctions proponents
rested upon their ability to draw an explicit connection between U.S.
domestic racial issues and the institutionalized racism of South Africa.
Anti-apartheid activists articulated a duty to act against South Africa
based upon ideals of democracy and justice—principles often cited by
conservative Republicans. For the first time, moderate and conservative

17. For more on Jackson's role, see Edmondson, "Black America," p. 192; Magubane,
Ties That Bind, p. 224; Baker, *United States and South Africa*, p. 30; and Anthony Sampson,
Black and Gold: Tycoons, Revolutionaries, and Apartheid (New York: Pantheon, 1987), p. 166.

18. Analysis of public opinion and voting patterns support this claim that a widely
shared belief in racial equality preceded broad-based demands for congressional sanctions. See Kevin A. Hill, "The Domestic Sources of Foreign Policymaking: Congressional
Voting and American Mass Attitudes toward South Africa," *International Studies Quarterly*
37 (June 1993), 195–214.

Republicans split over policy toward South Africa, resulting in Congress's rejection of the Reagan policy and the redefinition of U.S. interests in the region.

Constructive Engagement Rejected

The increasing importance of a norm of racial equality within foreign policy debates enabled opponents of the traditional U.S. policy to challenge the assumption that national interests were best served by supporting (or tolerating) white minority rule in South Africa. Distancing themselves from the appearance of tolerating racism led congressional representatives to advocate domestic South African reform. Because the Reagan administration policy of "constructive engagement" appeared to tolerate white minority rule, it became the target of domestic and congressional criticism.

Designed in 1981 by Reagan's assistant secretary of state for African affairs, Chester Crocker, constructive engagement meant "quiet diplomacy" based on three fundamental premises: that the U.S. could contribute to evolutionary change in South Africa; that some degree of outside intervention was necessary to promote "positive" movement in this direction; and that the U.S. could best exert its influence by rewarding significant reforms made by the white minority government.[19] Crocker rejected sanctions as punitive and counterproductive.

Despite strong continuities across administrations, significant differences distinguished constructive engagement from previous Republican approaches. Crocker believed that the white minority South African government was a reforming autocracy (and hence subject to influence) and that support for the government's efforts toward reform should be public.[20] Constructive engagement also differed from the lib-

19. For summaries of the tenets of constructive engagement, see Baker, *United States and South Africa,* pp. 8–9, and Coker, *United States and South Africa,* p. 155, as well as Crocker's original proposal in "South Africa: Strategy for Change," *Foreign Affairs* 59 (Winter 1980–81), 323–51. As is discussed below, Crocker desired South African domestic reform far less than Cuban troop withdrawal from Angola; see *High Noon.*

20. In contrast, Secretary of State Henry Kissinger in the 1970s presumed that the white South African government would not reform in response to external pressures (indeed, that it would continue to maintain internal stability indefinitely). He considered public dissociation from that government essential for minimizing the political costs of U.S. cooperation with it in pursuit of interests in the region. After the Portuguese coup in 1974 contradicted the premise that the whites were "here to stay," Kissinger stepped up covert interventions in the region (particularly Angola) in an effort to stave off perceived communist expansion among the newly independent former Portuguese

[handwritten margin notes: "left of econ / Liberal econ / view of reform ≠ / econ dev / pol / econ dev ≠ / pol reform"]

eral economic view of reform, which predominated in the Carter administration, because it was not based on the premise that evolutionary political reform would inevitably result from South Africa's economic development.[21] Thus Crocker aimed to avoid not only the sharp rhetoric and high visibility of the Carter administration but also the secret support given to South Africa under the Nixon administration. In promulgating constructive engagement, Crocker emphasized limitations on any U.S. attempt to influence change within South Africa. Such attempts, he argued, should be directed primarily at the white government, which could be swayed only if a friendly relationship were first established. Constructive engagement thus echoed the historical equation of strategic and economic interests, which primarily valued stability.

Despite his recognition of the need for some kind of domestic South African reform, Crocker's policy left the Reagan administration vulnerable to international and domestic criticism as it moved to strengthen previously severed ties with the South African government. To many observers, the policy of constructive engagement blatantly supported white minority rule. Even increased U.S. military cooperation with South Africa was documented, in secret policy documents that were leaked in 1981.[22] President Reagan's apparent personal sympathy for whites in South Africa further strengthened this impression (a view reinforced by his support from conservatives, especially in the South). Crocker's personal sympathies were also questioned in some circles because his wife was Rhodesian-born and they owned stock in companies operating in South Africa.[23]

---

colonies of Angola and Mozambique. On Kissinger's policy, see *National Security Study Memorandum 39: The Kissinger Study of Southern Africa*, ed. Mohamed A. El-Khawas and Barry Cohen (Westport, Conn.: Lawrence Hill, 1976).

21. The prosanctions perspective posited an essential connection between South Africa's economic system and its policies of apartheid, most specifically in the form of restrictions on labor mobility and heavy state involvement in the "private" sector. Therefore, it fundamentally contradicted the liberal economic view, as exemplified in the Sullivan Principles, that economic growth would benefit all South Africans (allegedly leading to expanded political opportunities). Until the public debates beginning in 1984, this liberal assumption had gone unchallenged within the policy-making process. On the differences between the liberal and structural views of economic change and apartheid reform, see Stanley B. Greenberg, "Economic Growth and Political Change: The South African Case," *Journal of Modern African Studies* 19 (December 1981), 667–704.

22. These documents were then printed in *TransAfrica News Report*, special edition (August 1981), and are reprinted in Baker, *United States and South Africa*, app. A, pp. 105–12.

23. Jesse Helms, in contrast, had attempted to block Crocker's nomination, fearing he was overly sympathetic to the black African perspective. On opposition to his nomination, see Crocker, *High Noon*.

The Reagan administration's reputation for supporting white minority rule was becoming entrenched. A strongly worded response by Democratic congressman William Gray (CBC member and author of sanctions legislation) to a Reagan press conference on 21 March 1985 commenting on the recent deaths of dozens of black South Africans, indicated a growing discontent with Reagan's insensitivity: "At best, I would describe [Reagan's] statements as symbolic of the worst kind of ignorance and insensitivity by anybody that I've ever seen in all my years in public office. At worst, I would have to say that they were racist. . . . [His comment] basically shows that the president sees [apartheid] only as a black-white issue, and he's on the side of white folks. And I think that's tragic, because its not a black-white issue. It's an issue of justice versus injustice."[24]

In response to increasing criticism that his administration supported white rule in South Africa, President Reagan finally made a speech denouncing apartheid on 10 December 1985, International Human Rights Day. He nevertheless justified the progress made through constructive engagement.[25] Particularly disturbing to his critics were Reagan's inaccurate assertions about South African support of the Allies during the two world wars; in fact, some members of the Afrikaner-dominated South African government had been imprisoned as Nazi sympathizers.

Characterizing support for South Africa as support for racism had serious political ramifications that became increasingly evident in the schism developing between the Reagan administration and Congress. For the first four years, most Republicans had given Crocker the benefit of the doubt (other opponents continued to criticize him for overlooking the issue of black political rights). This grace period, however,

---

24. Paula Hirschoff, "Interview: Congressman William H. Gray III," *Africa Report* 30 (May–June 1985), 50. To a question whether the administration would alter its policy in response to the continuing governmental violence against blacks, Reagan declared: "I think to put it that way—that they were simply killed and that the violence was coming totally from the law and order side—ignores the fact that there was rioting going on. . . . It is significant that some of those enforcing the law and using the guns were also black policemen." For his full comments, see "Remarks by President Reagan at a News Conference, March 21, 1985," in U.S. Department of State, *The United States and South Africa: U.S. Public Statements and Related Documents, 1977–1985* (Washington, D.C.: Government Printing Office, September 1985), doc. 158, p. 307.

25. Crocker also acknowledged both the damage from Reagan's insensitivity and the failure of constructive engagement to encourage South African reforms—in contrast to his self-proclaimed success in the regional dimension of his policy (*High Noon,* pp. 81, 231).

came to an end by late 1984, when both regional southern African and internal South African violence sharply increased.[26]

Particularly discontented were moderate Republicans who, in response to the growing impression of Reagan as insensitive to racial concerns, decided to voice their opposition openly. Crucial in creating bipartisan support for sanctions legislation, these former Reagan supporters became the cornerstone of the new congressional activism. But unlike activists with histories of interest in South African affairs, these moderates were influenced by a number of political contingencies in domestic U.S. politics that led them to reconsider national interests in, and policy toward, South Africa. The political linkage between domestic and international racial issues was the spark for this conservative reevaluation.

votes count

In part concerned by the electoral impact of domestic racial issues, centrist Republicans hoped to gain more support from middle-class blacks in their broader efforts to create a new style of Republican Party that would appeal to younger and Southern constituents.[27] Congressional representatives who previously had been uninterested in the details of foreign policies toward African countries now reined in the administration as their own concern for their party's image developed. Particularly surprising was Republican rather than Democratic attention to garnering black votes in a midterm election. Even more unusual was the adoption of a specific policy issue—whether or not to adopt sanctions against South Africa—as a focal point of posturing, as opposed to the vague "attentions" granted to "Africa" in previous electioneering. This new Republican concern had immediate effects on the sanctions debate, regardless of whether any individual representative was acting as a committed advocate of racial equality or more instrumentally in response to local political changes.

Public support for racial equality had become politically relevant for these moderate Republicans, leading them to promote anti-apartheid sanctions. In a much publicized letter to South African ambassador

26. The Nkomati and Lusaka accords between South Africa and its neighbors, which Crocker had held up as successes of constructive engagement, fell into disarray as South Africa adopted a more aggressive military strategy. On these accords and South Africa's broader regional policies, see James Barber and John Barratt, *South Africa's Foreign Policy: The Search for Status and Security 1945–1988* (Cambridge: Cambridge University Press, 1990), and chap. 5 above.

27. Baker, *United States and South Africa*, p. 36. Furthermore, analysis of public opinion and voting indicates that congressional representatives were responding to perceived black opinion but that there was no direct transmission of constituent attitudes to representatives; see Hill, "Domestic Sources," p. 210.

Fourie in December 1984, a group of these moderates expressed their concern about increasing violence in South Africa, going so far as to threaten support for partial sanctions if substantial change were not quickly forthcoming. In explaining his motivations for a move that circumvented the policy of his party's leader, Republican senator Robert Walker described the thinking behind his drafting of that letter:

> The letter grew out of discussions among several of us over several months. I found myself increasingly anxious to publicly express opposition to apartheid, and as I discussed it with my closest colleagues, I found that they too felt the time had come to have conservatives voice their repugnance regarding that policy of official segregation. We also were disturbed to see all conservatives lumped together as supporters of, or at least acquiescing to, apartheid. We decided to take steps to break this stereotype by taking a public step to show our disapproval. We set out to define ourselves as a group of conservatives who were clearly anti-apartheid. This, we felt, would send a signal to the South African government that it cannot count on all conservatives to "look the other way." We hoped this move would change the tenor of the debate not only in this country, but in South Africa as well.[28]

Thus moderate Republicans had come to agree with anti-apartheid activists that failure to respond harshly to South Africa's apartheid policies meant condoning racism. In the political climate of the mid-1980s, only the most conservative Republicans were deaf to such accusations.

As a result of increasing Republican support, bipartisan consensus on partial sanctions—as the policy that could most clearly and quickly demonstrate rejection of apartheid—emerged during 1985, in open opposition to the administration policy of constructive engagement. Supporting or even refusing to criticize South Africa had become politically unacceptable for all but the most conservative. Which specific policy would replace Reagan's, however, depended on subsequent debates over the importance of democracy for U.S. interests in the region.

28. Robert S. Walker, "A Conservative Viewpoint against Apartheid," *Africa Report* 30 (May–June 1985), 55. Sen. Richard G. Lugar similarly acknowledged that the linkage between South African and U.S. racial issues affected his thinking: "South Africa is a political issue full of symbolism and intense emotion for Americans. It is a foreign policy issue strongly tied to our own troubled racial history. . . . It evokes the memory of racial conflict in our own country and recalls how recently blacks were denied equal opportunity. Americans empathize with South African blacks and embrace them as suffering brothers"; see "Making Foreign Policy: The Congress and Apartheid," *Africa Report* 31 (September–October 1986), 33–34.

Economic Sanctions Adopted

The Reagan administration's failure to reach a sustainable compromise with Congress, most notably its inability to carry moderate Republicans, created unusual dissension over the broad definition of U.S. interests in southern Africa. Declining congressional support demonstrated that Reagan, unlike previous presidents, could no longer rely on orthodox assumptions that white minority rule in South Africa would protect U.S. strategic and economic interests. Promoting stability in the region, advocates of democracy argued, meant promoting substantial internal political reforms in South Africa. Anti-apartheid sanctions represented the most effective means of both pressuring the white minority government for reforms and signaling support for opponents of white rule. Support for sanctions, in other words, came to be equated with support for racial equality.

As moderate Republicans joined long-standing opponents of apartheid in articulating the view that an absence of South African reform actually promoted the spread of revolutionary ideas, they opened a broader discussion of the nature of U.S. interests. This new phase of debate centered around differing analyses of reform. Since traditional conservatives considered controlling the spread of communism to be the sole concern of U.S. policy, they viewed domestic reforms as inevitably destabilizing; black dissent was seen as trouble instigated by communist activists trained abroad, not as an autochthonous response to apartheid. In contrast, opponents of apartheid had always given greater credence to internal dissent. Most noteworthy in the 1980s was increasing recognition by moderate Republicans of the legitimacy of black South African demands for majority rule.

In no way giving up their vigilance against the spread of communism, these Republicans nevertheless did see that a narrow focus on strategic interests without an emphasis on democracy would mislead them about the serious implications of growing unrest in South Africa. Their assessment of the nature of the threat had changed now that Republicans acknowledged the idea of racial equality. Senator Walker, a leading Republican advocate of sanctions, observed,

> It hardly needs to be mentioned that South Africa plays a critical role through its opposition to communist expansion in sub-Saharan Africa. This has turned South Africa into a case where too many conservatives have turned a blind eye toward apartheid in the name of being pro-Western and anti-communist. . . . The option is a dismantling of apartheid that

moves South Africa toward human rights guarantees while preserving pro-Western government. In short, apartheid is eating away at the stability of South Africa. There is a danger that if it continues, the oppressed may seek liberation through violence and/or Marxism. We then could lose the very ally we regard as so vital. Better that we should help show the way toward reform.[29]

In other words, apartheid undermined South Africa's stability and consequently its value to the U.S. Seeing their own calls for partial sanctions as a warning to a "friend" rather than a threat to an "enemy," they hoped to encourage gradual reform to forestall a more violent revolution. Demands for democracy based on racial equality, therefore, were no longer dismissed as communism in disguise.

Chester Crocker's political analysis of both a communist threat and a need for reform paralleled that of moderate Republicans. His inflexibility toward their requests for policy modifications therefore requires explanation. Two factors help elucidate his intractability. First, in response to pressures from more conservative Reaganites, Crocker was attempting to stifle demands for severe actions against the ruling white South African government. And second, to attain a settlement on Namibia, the policy area that most interested him, he wanted a cooperative relationship with the South African government.[30] On the latter issue, Crocker differed with both moderate Republicans (who were more concerned with South African reform) and right-wing Republicans (who wanted a stronger reaction to the presence of Cuban troops in the region), leaving him open to attacks from all sides, not just from inveterate anti-apartheid activists. On balance, Crocker's emphasis on regional strategic interests, especially regarding Cuban troops in Angola, outweighed his moderate support for democratization.

Crucial to Crocker's preference for moderate reformers of apartheid was his tolerance solely for evolutionary, nonviolent change. Crocker minimized the importance both of black South African actors, such as

29. Walker, "Conservative View," pp. 54–55.

30. Rather than emphasize solely internal violence in South Africa, Crocker gave priority to the status of Namibia. Reflecting his concern over the spread of communism, much of Crocker's work focused on reaching a negotiated settlement between South Africa and Angola, linking Namibian independence to the withdrawal of Cuban troops from Angola. Crocker advocated closer ties with the Afrikaner government in order to enable a working relationship on the Namibian issue and, less urgently, to influence the direction and pace of domestic reforms (as evident in both the 1981 policy leaks to TransAfrica and his autobiography, *High Noon*). See also Baker, *United States and South Africa*, pp. 16, 41, and Minter, *King Solomon's Mines Revisited*, pp. 310–12.

the ANC, who supported faster change and of the degree of violence inherent in the system of apartheid. Sharing the conservative view that internal conflict was instigated by radical critics of white rule, Crocker concluded that violence could be controlled by a reformist South African government. Drawing sharply diverging conclusions from those internal conflicts, critics of this conservative perspective emphasized the role of the South African government in creating and perpetuating violence. In their view, not only did support for that government guarantee continued violence; slower reform ensured longer suffering, so stronger pressure on the South African government to make immediate and drastic changes was consequently the necessary and appropriate U.S. response. These diverging views of the relationship of violence and reform to U.S. interests became the fundamental conceptual division fueling the vociferous sanctions debates of the 1980s.

Following upon their December 1984 letter to the South African ambassador, a number of Republicans joined in sponsoring sanctions legislation in both the Senate and House. In 1985, the House passed sanctions legislation by a 295-127 margin, with the support of fifty-six Republicans. Republican senators Roth and McConnell introduced legislation in the Senate, where Reagan supporters Dole and Lugar became the key actors in an attempt to find a suitable compromise between Congress and the administration. Brokering an agreement to forestall restrictions on investments in South Africa, they convinced Reagan to abide by a much reduced package curtailing U.S. governmental loans, exports of computers to the South African military and police, transfers of nuclear-related technologies, and import of South African–made arms. Executive Order 12,532 also encouraged corporations to follow a code of conduct similar to the Sullivan Principles. Furthermore, an advisory committee was established to make additional recommendations in the future.[31]

This compromise, however, failed to placate critics either within the Republican Party or among other congressional members, who reiterated their proposals for sanctions legislation in the next session. As the administration tried to change the image but not the substance of its policy, violence continued to increase in southern Africa, with international criticism flaring as South Africa launched raids on neighboring

31. Executive Order 12,532 of September 9, 1985, "Prohibiting Trade and Certain Other Transactions Involving South Africa," reprinted in Department of State, *United States and South Africa* no. 176, pp. 365–68. Note that in its initial paragraph, the order refers to the UN Security Council arms embargo.

countries in May 1986. At the same time, the Commonwealth's Eminent Persons Group further substantiated impressions of P. W. Botha as intransigent by releasing its report calling for international sanctions.[32]

Ironically, Republican brokering for an executive order actually increased criticism of the administration, as it led to congressional discussions of which types of sanctions should be implemented; *whether* sanctions should be adopted was no longer questioned in Congress. With this shift in the terms of debate, the policy of constructive engagement finally died. Openly breaking with the conservatives within their party just before the November 1986 midterm elections, moderate Republicans, who had clearly decided that some sanctions were better than none, joined Democrats to override the president's veto of the Comprehensive Anti-Apartheid Act by overwhelming margins: 313-83 in the House and 78-21 in the Senate.

Major provisions of the act, going beyond the previous executive order, included restrictions on new investments in South Africa, stronger restrictions on governmental loans, imports from South Africa (including gold coins), trade assistance, and tourism promotion, as well as the elimination of preferential taxation agreements. Furthermore, the act made mandatory a code of conduct, based upon the much vaunted Sullivan Principles, for U.S. corporations operating in South Africa. Additional "positive" measures such as educational aid and legal assistance were included, as was the possibility of further sanctions after a follow-up report from the president within twelve months. The Comprehensive Anti-Apartheid Act also established conditions for the removal of these sanctions. These included South Africa's releasing political prisoners, lifting the state of emergency, ending bans on political activity, repealing the Group Areas Act and Population Registration Act, and entering into good faith negotiations with representatives of the black majority.[33]

Adoption of sanctions thus marked an unusual bipartisan consensus among members of Congress—and the public—that promoting racial equality and democracy in South Africa was a prerequisite for attaining its other national interests. While conflicts remained over policies toward the region as a whole, including Namibia and Angola, sanctions

32. See Commonwealth Group of Eminent Persons, *Mission to South Africa: The Commonwealth Report* (London: Penguin, 1986), and chap. 4 above.

33. The 99th Congress, "The Comprehensive Anti-Apartheid Act of 1986," Public Law 99-440, 2 October 1986, *Statutes at Large* no. 100, pp. 1086–116.

marked a dramatic shift in the direction of U.S. policy and further weakened the administration's strategic perspective.

By legally institutionalizing sanctions, the Comprehensive Anti-Apartheid Act inaugurated a period of more consistent U.S. opposition to white minority rule. Evaluating enforcement of the specific provisions of the sanctions package in 1987, Secretary of State Shultz's advisory report recommended policy measures that reinforced the act: distancing the U.S. government from the white regime, strengthening its own ties with the black opposition, and increasing assistance to South Africa's neighboring states. No longer treating the ANC as a terrorist organization to be shunned, Shultz even met with ANC president Oliver Tambo in 1987.[34] Furthermore, the Bush administration abided by the act's conditions for lifting sanctions, even after Britain and the European Economic Community announced their intention to revoke their sanctions following Nelson Mandela's release from prison in 1990. Only after President de Klerk's 1991 reforms did the United States lift sanctions.

Congressional action also strengthened the global momentum for sanctions. Shortly after passage of the U.S. anti-apartheid act, the Commonwealth and Europeans adopted economic sanctions, and Japan adopted bilateral restrictions following the U.S. lead.[35] Thus only after transnational pressures produced a foreign policy that supported racial equality did U.S. sanctions function the way hegemonic regime theorists would expect.

The United States' adoption of anti-apartheid sanctions was surprising given the historical continuity in its support for South Africa. Prior to the mid-1980s, policy toward Africa was generally insulated from domestic pressures as the United States pursued its strategic and economic interests. Access to minerals and markets seemed ensured under conservative South African governments. But in response to growing vocal public support for racial equality and reform in South Africa, top policy makers in the mid-1980s disrupted this easy correspondence between U.S. interests and white minority rule. Redefining U.S. interests in the region to include support for racial equality, indeed as a prereq-

34. The act is noteworthy for its explicit antagonism to the ANC as a "terrorist" organization; see Thomas J. Redden, Jr., "The U.S. Comprehensive Anti-Apartheid Act of 1986: Anti-Apartheid or Anti-African National Congress?" *African Affairs* 87 (October 1988), 595–605.

35. In addition to chaps. 4 and 7, see Richard J. Payne, "Japan's South Africa Policy: Political Rhetoric and Economic Realities," *African Affairs* 86 (April 1987), 167–78.

uisite for—rather than an alternative to—strategic and economic interests, congressional leaders initiated sanctions against South Africa.

Structural theories that consider only material interests cannot explain the dramatic change in U.S. policy toward South Africa in the 1980s. U.S. sanctions policy demonstrated the strength of a commitment to racial equality, both domestically and in South Africa. Furthermore, regime theories, which emphasize the role of multilateral institutional constraints, might have predicted the United States to lead the global sanctions policies; but rather than initiating global agitation over apartheid and promoting international sanctions, U.S. policy instead responded to transnational pressures. Even while Congress rejected constructive engagement, the Reagan administration blocked UN Security Council sanctions. Only after the anti-apartheid movement succeeded in generating the Comprehensive Anti-Apartheid Act did U.S. actions reinforce global momentum toward sanctions. In other words, this case shows that even if a hegemon's sanctions are helpful in isolating a target state, analysts should not follow realists in presuming that they are essential.

Equally important, however, U.S. sanctions policy calls into question the realist view that norms can function only as weak ethical constraints on the pursuit of more fundamental material interests. Congressional leaders did not simply claim that racial equality had become more important than strategic minerals or profits to be made in a free-market system. Rather, they recognized that stability in southern Africa would be best ensured through the promotion of majority rule. Racial equality became a prerequisite for attaining material goals. The norm redefined U.S. interests.

CHAPTER SEVEN

Britain

Britain maintained strong strategic and economic ties with South Africa in the postwar era. Material interest calculations would lead us to expect Britain to oppose calls by both domestic actors and international organizations for sanctions. From this perspective, the anti-apartheid movement's inability to generate sanctions through domestic mobilization in Britain, as in the United States, would not be surprising. Britain's consistent rejection of UN and Commonwealth sanctions further conforms with conventional expectations.

According to these structural theories, however, multilateral cooperation is unlikely to succeed without hegemonic leadership and is even less likely to constrain the policies of great powers. Yet Commonwealth members adopted multilateral sanctions despite British objections, and Britain even modified its policies to include voluntary measures. As anti-apartheid pressures escalated in 1986, the Thatcher government attempted to deflect Commonwealth criticism by shifting focus to the European Community. But as the Europeans also moved toward sanctions, Britain modified its South Africa stance, contrary to its stated policy as well as its material interests. And yet its policy did not appear to respond to changes in material costs and benefits; it had little to lose by withdrawing from the Commonwealth and little reason to expect the Europeans to enforce compliance with a multilateral policy.

Thus this case does not fit a regime theory emphasis on international institutions as constraints, if costs and benefits are calculated only in military and economic terms. Rather, in both the Commonwealth and the European Community, Britain tolerated the costs of bending to anti-apartheid pressures in order to gain the intangible benefits of supporting racial equality. First, I explain that internal anti-apartheid activists were ineffective because of the absence of a domestic discourse of racial equality and the institutional insulation of Britain's foreign policy–making process. Then I explore international pressures through the Commonwealth and European Community. Britain's policy did not shift as dramatically as that of the United States, but, I argue, compromises—particularly partial economic "measures" and support for the Frontline States—indicate the strength of normative constraint. Reputation matters.

INEFFECTIVE DOMESTIC DEMANDS FOR RACIAL EQUALITY

Despite steadily increasing international and domestic protest against apartheid, Britain defended its strong strategic and economic ties. Yet because of the porous nature of its sovereignty, a legacy of its imperial and Commonwealth history, Britain has often pursued global, rather than strictly national, interests. As a first step in understanding British policy toward South Africa, we must thus explore whether and how its leaders articulated national interests in the face of anti-apartheid pressures. Unlike President Reagan in the United States, Prime Minister Thatcher successfully deflected domestic demands for sanctions.

Transnational Origins of Anti-Apartheid Pressures

During Britain's imperial days, activists seeking to improve political and economic conditions for its African subjects targeted London. Among the first to do so were South African blacks. The founders of the African National Congress (established in 1912) protested the creation of a new Dominion, the Union of South Africa, that marginalized indigenous Africans. Despite their failure to influence the settlement of the Anglo-Boer war, demands for British assistance increased after the two world wars. An influx of South African exiles arrived in Britain following the implementation of apartheid in 1948. As the core of a nascent and growing anti-apartheid movement, these exiles (and their allies) hoped to influence international actors, especially the United Nations and the Commonwealth, to implement sanctions against South

Africa.[1] London's importance for the anti-apartheid movement was part of the growth of the British capital as a center for African liberation groups from other colonies as well.

Once established in London, South African exiles maintained political ties among a number of support groups within mainstream British society, including labor unions and factions within the churches, as well as the Labour and Liberal parties. Initially this coalition joined in a one-month boycott of South African products in 1960. Paralleling general changes in European social movements, the anti-apartheid movement grew more militant in the 1960s, expanding its political network to include more radical allies such as the student movement, which continued anti-apartheid demonstrations during the 1970s and 1980s.

Support for sanctions became more visible and vocal. The British Council of Churches, for example, came out in favor of economic disengagement in 1979 after almost twenty years of fractious debate, and the Trade Union Congress reached an agreement in 1985 with nine leading retailers to remove South African goods from their shelves.[2] By the 1980s, a substantial portion of British society sympathized with the sanctions cause. Public opinion polls taken between November 1985 and July 1986 showed a swing in favor of tougher measures: the proportion of those who thought that British policy was not strong enough increased from 42 percent to 56 percent, while 65 percent expressed dissatisfaction with Prime Minister Thatcher's handling of the issue.[3]

Despite its increasingly formal political ties among Liberals and Labour, as well as the prevalence of demonstrations, the anti-apartheid movement showed little influence on British foreign policy. Numerous factors, relating to both the nature of the movement and the broader political constraints of the British parliamentary system, explain this ineffectiveness. For example, anti-apartheid activists pursued particular aims (education, international promotion of sanctions) rather than

1. Dennis Austin, *Britain and South Africa* (Oxford: Oxford University Press, 1966), p. 13.

2. James Barber, *The Uneasy Relationship: Britain and South Africa* (London: Heinemann, 1983), pp. 57, 75; Joseph Hanlon and Roger Omond, *The Sanctions Handbook* (London: Penguin, 1987), pp. 135–40.

3. *The Times* (London), 1 August 1986, quoted in Colin Legum, *Battlefronts of Southern Africa* (New York: Africana, 1988), p. 430. *The Economist* (London), however, added that "solid majorities" did not favor sanctions on air links, sports, or general trade (16 August 1986, 29).

function as a political pressure group specifically within Britain.[4] While widespread, vocal opposition to apartheid persisted, sanctions never became a salient electoral issue.[5]

Unlike in the United States, in Britain the issues of domestic racial discrimination and apartheid remained politically separate. Controversy over racism revolved around two main issues: immigration policy and police violence.[6] Antagonism toward racial minorities was not simply a fringe radical-right sentiment. Since the early 1960s, both Tory and Labour governments had implemented restrictive immigration policies. In the 1970s Conservative members of Parliament targeted the immigration issue in part hoping to co-opt the far-right (National Front) vote. Inner city riots in 1981 exacerbated antiblack sentiment, often expressed as part of broader xenophobic attitudes. Even among Labour politicians who were sensitive to issues of racial equality, a focus on class generally prevailed.

In addition, despite their increasing voice within the Labour Party, blacks remained outside the most powerful political institutions, with the exception of a very few members of Parliament. Grassroots organizations remained both locally based and oriented toward specific issues. Intermediary institutions (that is, between local councils and national Parliament) offered little alternative; the Thatcher government completely dissolved the Greater London Council, one such intermediary institution under Labour control. Thus although politicized and active at the local level, few black Britons advanced to the national level, and no arguments directly linked the apartheid issue to these domestic political debates.

Finally, the Thatcher government's persistent efforts to break labor unions substantially weakened the opposition Labour Party and the Trade Union Congress, traditionally the anti-apartheid movement's most powerful allies.[7] Thus Neil Kinnock's announcement at the Octo-

4. Barber, *Uneasy Relationship*, pp. 60–61; he also sees this as an explanation for its persistence (p. 65).

5. Ibid., p. 58. In addition, it is rare for a foreign policy issue to become salient in British electoral politics. See James Barber, *Who Makes British Foreign Policy?* (Milton Keynes: Open University Press, 1976), esp. chaps. 9 and 12.

6. For discussion of these issues, see Peter Fryer, *Staying Power: The History of Black People in Britain* (London: Pluto Press, 1984); *Race, Government, and Politics in Britain*, ed. Zig Layton-Henry and Paul B. Rich (London: Macmillan, 1986); *Black Politics in Britain*, ed. Harry Goulbourne (Aldershot: Avebury, 1990); and Zig Layton-Henry, *The Politics of Race in Britain* (London: George Allen and Unwin, 1984).

7. Thatcher came to power during the 1979 coal strike and proceeded to break the

ber 1986 Labour Party conference that he supported full sanctions was unlikely to influence Thatcher's stance.[8] Even if Labour had actually come to power in the 1980s, it is doubtful that policy would have shifted dramatically; historically, Labour governments rarely altered the direction of prevailing foreign policy.[9] Having Labour as an ally during the 1980s consequently remained of dubious value for the anti-apartheid movement as it was unable to advance the cause of sanctions within Parliament. Despite decades of activism, the government stayed insulated from transnational pressures.

Economic and Strategic Counterarguments

The substance of the counterarguments against sanctions further hampered British anti-apartheid activists and their allies. Rather than treating sanctions solely in terms of racism or long-term interests, domestic debate focused on loss of jobs. Indeed, many Labour as well as Tory politicians agreed that Britain could not afford an economic war with South Africa.[10] Proponents of sanctions had to defend themselves against assertions that sanctions would cost many jobs within Britain (during a period of high unemployment), and Thatcher strove for the moral high ground by declaring her refusal to exacerbate British or

mine workers' union. With the progressive decline in union strength, she was able to dismantle the previous "corporatist" nature of British politics. Declaring hers a politics of "conviction," Thatcher broke with the traditional politics of consensus. In so doing, she pushed Labour (and center Liberals) even further from influencing policies. On Thatcherism, see Peter Jenkins, *Mrs. Thatcher's Revolution: The Ending of the Socialist Era* (London: Pan, 1987). For a historical overview of Labour and union support for sanctions, see Hanlon and Omond, *Sanctions Handbook*, pp. 135–40.

8. Even Labour's stand on the issue of deployment of nuclear weapons, amid public protest organized by the Campaign for Nuclear Disarmament, failed to influence Thatcher; the government's insulation from public sentiment on the sanctions issue was hardly surprising in comparison. These are examples of the insignificance of "promotional" (as opposed to "protective") pressure groups in influencing British policies. And even when Parliament does debate foreign affairs, party loyalty prevails; see Barber, *Who Makes British Foreign Policy?* pp. 70–71, 25.

9. Barber claims that Labour governments are often indistinguishable from Tory; foreign policy is generally consistent, reflecting different emphases rather than directions. This is partly explained by divisions between "left wing" and "realist" views within the Labour Party; in foreign affairs the latter have always prevailed. Continuity within the civil service also promotes continuity in policy. British foreign policy has consistently been made by incremental decisions, not new initiatives, regardless of the party in power. See Barber, *Who Makes British Foreign Policy?* p. 25; Hanlon and Omond, *Sanctions Handbook*, p. 137.

10. Barber, *Uneasy Relationship*, p. 90.

black South African unemployment.[11] Concerned about economic ramifications, the business community initially shared Thatcher's antisanctions perspective.

As anti-apartheid pressure increased, British business, in collaboration with their South African associates, countered by organizing interest groups, most notably the South Africa Foundation and the United Kingdom–South Africa Trade Association (UKSATA). These groups used tactics such as sponsoring visits to South Africa, which often included interviews with moderate antisanctions blacks.[12] Direct contacts also enhanced the implicit and explicit exchange of views between government and business, and Tory leaders often owned stock in firms with operations in South Africa or sat on the boards of such companies.

But as unrest in South Africa spread, a number of companies came under increasing pressure from British divestment protesters, whose greatest success was the withdrawal of Barclays Bank on "economic" grounds—which included decreasing profits at home due to protesters' boycotts. In March 1985, top business leaders met in secret with their U.S. and South African counterparts, at the instigation of the Reverend Leon Sullivan (author of the Sullivan Principles code of conduct for businesses operating in South Africa) and Conservative former British prime minister Edward Heath.[13]

Joining with numerous South African and U.S. corporations, many

11. Hanlon and Omond, *Sanctions Handbook*, pp. 228–42; Margaret Thatcher, *The Downing Street Years* (New York: HarperCollins, 1993), pp. 512–24.

12. The South Africa Foundation was established in 1959 to strengthen South Africa's international economic ties. With offices in London, Bonn, Paris, and Washington, it received support from 80 percent of South Africa's leading mining, industrial, and commercial firms. It concentrated its efforts on top-level contacts with businesses, politicians, the media, and academics; it produced the monthly *South Africa Foundation News* and the quarterly *South Africa International.* Its basic messages were that South Africa was misunderstood overseas, its economy was strong, and incremental reform was desirable. UKSATA, founded in 1966 as an offshoot of the Confederation of British Industry, worked more "quietly and discreetly." One of its members called it the de facto "commercial arm of the South African embassy," and it had ties with the British Foreign Office. Its head, John McQuiggan, was said to sound more conservative than the Pretoria government. See Barber, *Uneasy Relationship*, pp. 68–73, and Anthony Sampson, *Black and Gold: Tycoons, Revolutionaries, and Apartheid* (New York: Pantheon, 1987), pp. 89–90, 174–75, 207.

13. Those present included Sir Peter Baxendall of Shell, Sir Peter Walters of British Petroleum, Sir Tim Bevans of Barclays Bank, Sir Alistair Frame of Rio-Tinto-Zinc, Roger Smith of General Motors, Rawleigh Warner of Mobil, and John Reed of Citibank. The South African leaders present (including Tony Bloom of Premier Group and Judge Steyn of the Urban Foundation) were most radical, while the British chairmen saw no need for bold commitments. They could agree merely to a weak communiqué of "common concern," which was never issued (Sampson, *Black and Gold*, p. 173).

key business leaders established preliminary contacts with African National Congress representatives in October 1985 and publicized their efforts to enhance conditions for their black employees within South Africa, a year before the British government followed suit.[14] Thus even South African sympathizers within the business community were growing disenchanted with Thatcher's policies. But rather than try to change government policy, they acted unilaterally. Thatcher's policies were clearly not being driven by business interests—or not as perceived by British businesses.[15]

The South African issue remained within the purview of the cabinet and Thatcher personally, as is traditional in British foreign-policy decision making.[16] Thatcher also tended to segregate issues among departments, operating under the principle that "the Ministry of Agriculture looks after farmers, the Foreign Office looks after foreigners."[17] Compartmentalization and centralization enhanced her already substantial insulation from domestic pressures (even from business groups) while making individual contacts and personal preferences more salient.[18] Thatcher's concern over the perceived spread of communism into South Africa explains much of Britain's unwillingness to implement sanctions. Indeed, in July 1986 Thatcher proclaimed, "It is absurd that people should be prepared to put increasing power into the hands of the Soviet Union on the grounds that they disapprove of apartheid in South Africa."[19]

Thatcher firmly established Britain's reputation as South Africa's

14. Not all business interests joined in tolerance for the ANC. Stalwart supporters of South Africa opposed sanctions through the newly formed British Industry Committee on South Africa, established in January 1986 to galvanize and publicize that support. Secret meetings among top business leaders continued in 1986, but no common ground was established (ibid., pp. 196, 207, 212).

15. Thatcher had already adamantly rejected the politics of consensus, and apartheid was no exception. Jenkins, *Mrs. Thatcher's Revolution,* chap. 3; Thatcher, *Downing Street Years,* chap. 17.

16. Although the key actors vary somewhat by specific policy, those consistently most important have been the foreign secretary and defense minister, in addition to the prime minister. Although officially head of state, the queen does not play an overt role in policy making. Political analysts differ over whether the prime minister dominates or mediates within the cabinet; personality, they agree, is often crucial. See Barber, *Who Makes British Foreign Policy?*

17. Norman Tebbit, quoted in Jenkins, *Mrs. Thatcher's Revolution,* p. 285.

18. Barber, *Who Makes British Foreign Policy?* p. 18. At least until 1983, policy makers tried to treat each aspect of South Africa policy as a distinct issue, whereas the anti-apartheid movement tried to link them all to apartheid (Barber, *Uneasy Relationship,* p. 84).

19. Quoted from Sampson, *Black and Gold,* p. 215; this perspective also appears throughout Thatcher, *Downing Street Years,* chap.17.

strongest supporter. Like her conservative U.S. ally, Ronald Reagan, she adamantly supported "persuasion": she insisted that continued relations with the South African government would provide the most leverage. She claimed a special relationship with President P. W. Botha, based on forthright exchanges devoid of moral rhetoric, and believed her influence in the direction of reforms would be strongest if threats and confrontation were avoided. Furthermore, Thatcher adopted the liberal economic argument that enlightened business would be the appropriate vehicle for reform, and her views were reinforced by visits to 10 Downing Street of South African opponents of sanctions, including Zulu chief Mangosuthu Buthelezi, parliamentarian Helen Suzman, and industrialist Harry Oppenheimer. Meanwhile, Thatcher steadfastly rejected contacts with black "terrorists" such as the ANC, exiled activists in London were shunned, and in Johannesburg internal activists were ignored at the British Embassy.[20]

Both the South African government and anti-apartheid activists saw Thatcher as a staunch supporter of the National Party regime. Internal pressures and even divisions within the business community had failed to sway her government to change its policies toward South Africa. Thus Britain's gradual acceptance, between 1985 and 1987, of restrictive "measures" represented a departure from the government's previous pronouncements and actions. Given Thatcher's persistent rejection of sanctions, as well as her decisive role in policy making, Britain's adoption of partial measures at the height of the sanctions debates indicates the effectiveness of international pressures.

ADAPTING TO MULTILATERAL PRESSURES

The gradual British acceptance of partial sanctions developed out of concomitant and spiraling pressures from three different directions. Most audible were voices in the Commonwealth, including fellow conservatives such as Prime Minister Mulroney of Canada. Increasingly, even fellow European countries, which had previously followed British initiative on multilateral EEC policy toward South Africa, pressed for sanctions. As international criticism escalated, divisions within Thatcher's own cabinet also emerged, finally bringing her to adopt sanctions and provide aid to the Frontline States, despite her vocal objections.

20. Sampson, *Black and Gold,* p. 216; Thatcher, *Downing Street Years,* chap. 17.

Commonwealth Sanctions

In the postwar period, Britain's substantial economic and strategic interests ensured continuity in its policy toward South Africa. Over the decades, successive governments followed tactics of "marginal adjustments" rather than taking new initiatives.[21] Consistently blocking strong action within the United Nations and only begrudgingly accepting South Africa's rejection from the Commonwealth, Britain retained strong political as well as private economic ties. South Africa did not, for example, lose preferential trading status when it withdrew from the Commonwealth.[22] Shifts in this relatively consistent British support came primarily at times of focused pressure from within the Commonwealth.

The most notable example of modification during a Tory government was the 1971 attempt to sell banned arms to South Africa. Britain claimed that these sales not only were justified under the long-standing Simonstown defense agreement but were also essential for defense of the Cape route and beneficial for the British economy. Arguing also for a distinction between weapons for external security and for domestic repression, the Conservative government attempted to separate the question of apartheid from issues of national defense. As a result, it came under severe recrimination at the 1971 Commonwealth conference in Singapore. Prime Minister Heath backed down under these attacks, canceling the intended sales.[23]

A second notable precedent for Commonwealth influence on Tory policy was Rhodesia. Neither Labour nor Tory governments would risk harming relations with South Africa in order to gain a settlement on Rhodesia. Although Labour prime minister Harold Wilson favored sanctions after the Rhodesian Unilateral Declaration of Independence, he rejected strong enforcement measures such as a blockade; nor were there any serious attempts to stop South Africa from evading restrictions. In the area of sanctions against South Africa itself, Labour did

21. Barber, *Uneasy Relationship*, p. 6.

22. Geoff Berridge, *Economic Power in Anglo-South African Diplomacy: Simonstown, Sharpeville, and After* (London: Macmillan, 1981).

23. Britain ended up sending helicopters for use on frigates; sales had previously been limited to spare parts. See James Barber and John Barratt, *South Africa's Foreign Policy 1945–1988: The Search for Status and Security* (Cambridge: Cambridge University Press, 1990), pp. 157–58. Ironically, in the debates of the mid-1980s, Heath (whom Thatcher had ousted as party leader) led a prosanctions faction within the Conservative Party. On debates over weapons for external defense versus internal repression, see chap. 3 above on the UN arms embargoes.

little to break with the precedent of blocking international measures and gradually allowed the United States to take the initiative.

However, in 1979, concerted Commonwealth efforts prevented Thatcher from officially recognizing the "internal settlement" government (which, while nominally led by an African, fell short of instituting universal suffrage). The combined forces of Commonwealth secretary-general Ramphal, select prime ministers, and her own foreign secretary, Lord Carrington, prevailed in convincing Thatcher to support one more (in the end successful) constitutional conference to settle the issue of Rhodesian and Zimbabwean independence to the satisfaction of the international community.[24]

As in 1971 and 1979, British policy toward southern Africa in the mid-1980s confronted strong criticism from the Commonwealth. At the Nassau meeting of the Commonwealth in October 1985, Thatcher for the first time came under concerted pressure to agree to a package of sanctions against South Africa from a new array of voices including Canada and Australia. Even states that either had previously sympathized with the British position, such as Singapore, or now stood to bear the costs of sanctions, such as Swaziland and Lesotho, left Thatcher isolated against sanctions. Member states chose Canada's Mulroney and India's Gandhi to lobby Thatcher personally, hoping to win agreement as on the Rhodesia issue at the Lusaka summit.[25]

While resisting personal pressures, Thatcher nevertheless did agree to a "tiny" compromise of very limited "signs and gestures," which she adamantly refused to call "sanctions"; these included restricting the import of Krugerrands and withdrawing of official trade promotion. She even declared a victory over her opposition, claiming that "they joined me."[26] Thatcher was heavily criticized after the meeting for her combative stance.

In attempting to reach a Commonwealth consensus and avoid dead-

24. However, note that Thatcher claims she influenced Commonwealth leaders, rather than vice versa (*Downing Street Years*, chap. 3). See chaps. 4 and 8 for more on the Lusaka summit meeting.

25. The precedent of Lusaka may actually have hindered efforts to persuade Thatcher. In Stephen Chan's analysis, Thatcher resisted calls for sanctions as a point of pride—particularly as advocates used the same method of intensive informal lobbying. Chan also saw Thatcher's stubbornness as an error of judgment that prevented her from seizing the initiative to attain a limited sanctions package along the lines of Reagan's presidential directive; see "The Commonwealth and South Africa," *New Zealand International Review* 11 (September–October 1986), p. 24. Compare Thatcher's own description of the Nassau meeting in *Downing Street Years*, pp. 516–19.

26. *The Times*, 22 October 1985, 1; Thatcher, *Downing Street Years*, pp. 518–19.

lock on sanctions, Australia's Prime Minister Hawke presented the idea of sending an Eminent Persons Group to try to reason the South African government into dialogue. Thatcher, while intially cool to the idea, eventually conceded (not only under threats of Nigerian retaliation against Britain but also amid rumors that other Commonwealth members were prepared to proceed even without her).[27] Member states nominated a variety of individuals; Britain nominated Lord Barber, who was the chairman of Standard Chartered Bank (which had substantial interests in South Africa) and a former Tory chancellor of the exchequer. The appointment of an apparently "safe" delegate, together with phrasing in the accord allowing for the possible consideration of further measures in six months (after the EPG was to report), reassured Thatcher that the EPG would serve as a stalling device.[28]

To her (and others') surprise, when the EPG issued its report in June 1986, Lord Barber went along with the consensus, which was more critical of South Africa than had been expected.[29] The report argued that international sanctions against South Africa were necessary to bring an end to apartheid. In so doing, it adamantly refuted Thatcher's argument that South Africa was reforming and willing to negotiate. The findings of the mission presented the Botha government as draconian and inflexible; even while the mission was touring South Africa to promote its "negotiating concept," the South African government bombed three neighboring Frontline States. Furthermore, the report stated that negotiated settlement would be impossible without the participation of the ANC, refuting yet another of Thatcher's tenets. Such critical findings could only help those calling on Thatcher for further concessions.

Criticism of Thatcher hardened during the weeks leading up to the August 1986 Commonwealth minisummit in London, at which the EPG report was to be heard. But whereas previous differences of opinion had been privately voiced, these disputes became public. Most controversial were the rumors in July that Queen Elizabeth was worried

27. *The Times*, 18, 19, and 22 October 1985, 1. In contrast, Thatcher describes herself as one of a number of people who endorsed the EPG idea; see *Downing Street Years*, p. 518.

28. Lord Barber was expected to be "cautious" since he had previously shown little interest in black Africa despite regular visits to South Africa, where he had numerous business and personal contacts (Sampson, *Black and Gold*, p. 219). Thatcher had originally wanted her foreign secretary, Sir Geoffrey Howe, to lead the mission.

29. Commonwealth Eminent Persons Group on Southern Africa, *Mission to South Africa: The Commonwealth Report* (London: Penguin, 1986).

about the impact that the prime minister's rejection of sanctions would have on the Commonwealth. Controversy raged over both the "leak" from the palace to the *Sunday Times* (20 July) and the content of the criticism. The precise motivation behind the leak, whether by Howe and Deputy Prime Minister Lord Whitelaw, the Commonwealth secretary-general, or the queen herself, was never determined. The effect was to escalate demands for Thatcher to be more receptive to Commonwealth views.[30]

A number of member countries expressed their views symbolically by boycotting the Commonwealth Games in Edinburgh that same month. They exerted pressure in more substantial ways as well. Along with its initiation of the Edinburgh sports boycott, Nigeria threatened to suspend its Commonwealth membership should the minisummit fail to agree on sanctions. Moreover, it threatened to withdraw if Thatcher blocked EEC sanctions in September. Others considered following suit. With U.S. sanctions ever more likely as well, the stage was set for convincing Thatcher at the London meeting.

Dismayed by the EPG's failure to propel the South African government into negotiations, the Commonwealth—with the exception of Britain—agreed to implement partial sanctions as suggested at the Nassau meeting. In a precedent-setting dissent, Thatcher appended her own position to the Commonwealth accord. She also, however, announced a voluntary ban on new investment and on the promotion of tourism. In a sudden switch at the end of the meeting, she declared not only these "measures" but also her willingness to go along with any European trade restrictions on iron, steel, and coal.[31]

While passage of these measures relieved the immediate pressure, demands for additional actions continued. But Thatcher distanced her-

30. The issue arose of whether it was appropriate for the queen's political views to become public. Her views should, by custom, be expressed privately. Yet as the head of state for many Commonwealth member countries as well, the queen's position was ambiguous; some argued that it was legitimate, in Commonwealth terms, for the queen to express such opinions (for example, see Chan, "Commonwealth and South Africa," p. 23). It is common knowledge that the queen plays a role behind the scenes within the Commonwealth, in addition to her figurehead role: see Stephen Chan, "The Commonwealth and the Future," *New Zealand International Review* 11 (November–December 1986, 18.

31. Thatcher, *Downing Street Years*, pp. 520–22. She also threatened, however, to withdraw these concessions if they were derided as insufficient or if her sincerity were questioned; see Peter Lyon, "The August Mini-Summit and After," *The Round Table* 300 (October 1986), 308.

self even further from Commonwealth consensus.[32] Revealing a significant disagreement with her foreign secretary, Thatcher continued to denounce the ANC as a terrorist organization—while Howe and his assistant, Lynda Chalker, had begun meeting with the ANC in September 1986. Up until 1987, while most of the world, including South African business executives and politicians, had recognized the importance of the ANC as a legitimate partner in any negotiated settlement, Thatcher continued to reject it as communist and terrorist. Even after the EPG reported the inflexibility of the South African regime, Thatcher steadfastly proclaimed progress in its reforms. Continuing to hold her own view of the South African situation, Thatcher replaced her foreign secretary with a new one less likely to dispute her views.[33]

Thatcher supported measures such as additional aid to the Frontline States, as well as minimal sanctions, in attempts to stave off more substantial sanctions. The Foreign Office issued a pamphlet entitled "British Aid to Southern Africa" a few months before the Commonwealth meeting that presaged what would be Thatcher's renewed emphasis on using "positive" rather than "punitive" measures. The British government announced, "Opposition to sanctions does not imply acceptance of apartheid. . . . But we are trying, in a positive and practical way, to help promote the peaceful and prosperous development of States in the region, and reduce their economic dependence on South Africa."[34] Such a shift paralleled the increasingly regional orientation of the EEC. It also marked the only area of apparent agreement between Britain and other Commonwealth members, in a meeting otherwise dominated by Thatcher's unprecedented dissent.

Notably, Thatcher consented at the summit to support more aid to the Frontline States, particularly Mozambique, despite her rejection of the newly established Committee of Foreign Ministers that was to guide future Commonwealth policy toward southern Africa. Rarely, however, did Thatcher acknowledge the influence of outside pressures or the degree to which her policy had substantively changed. Yet similar shifts are also evident in her response to pressures within the EEC.

32. Stephen Chan, "Margaret Thatcher's Commonwealth Stance: Wielding a Blunt Instrument," *New Zealand International Review* 13 (January–February 1988), 8.

33. John Major had no foreign affairs experience, and during the 1989 Commonwealth summit in Kuala Lumpur, he was clearly Thatcher's subordinate; see Stephen Chan, "Mrs. Thatcher and Her Foreign Secretaries," *New Zealand International Review* 15 (January–February 1990), 10.

34. Quoted in Peter Lyon, "The Commonwealth and the Vancouver Meeting," *The Round Table* 305 (January 1988), 3.

European Sanctions

While dissent from former colonies had become a feature of discord in the Commonwealth, criticism about South Africa from allied Western industrialized countries in the mid-1980s was new. Even other European countries, which earlier had taken their cue from Britain, now initiated changes in their own bilateral relations and rallied for multilateral EEC sanctions.[35]

In the late 1970s, Britain had taken the lead in shaping joint European policy toward South Africa by advocating the institution of a code of conduct for business (similar to the Sullivan Principles), along the lines of one already adopted in 1974 under Wilson's Labour government. Building on its own experience in deflecting domestic criticism and hiding behind a concerted European response, in July 1977 Britain floated the idea of an EEC Code of Conduct, which also garnered support from West Germany. After a quick drafting (to which unions and the European Parliament objected because they were not consulted), the code was adopted in September 1977. Some countries, particularly the Netherlands, Ireland, and Denmark, advocated mandatory measures instead, but most supported the voluntary code.

Less enthusiastic about the code than her predecessors, Thatcher did not promote its periodic revision and strengthening as had originally been intended; monitoring remained nationally rather than EEC-based, and no enforcement procedures existed. Bilateral trade with South Africa continued while the code had no visible influence on apartheid. Its apparent ineffectiveness, combined with President Botha's extensive 1984 tour of European capitals (the first such tour since 1961), made European trading partners a prime target of renewed calls for international sanctions.

By 1985 Europe's previous complacency and consensus were replaced by diverging responses to the escalating violence and repression within South Africa. Following a Dutch initiative, the Community announced in July that it would establish a committee to report on making the code tougher. In the meantime, however, France preempted such a moderate response by unilaterally withdrawing its ambassador from South Africa and prohibiting new French investments there.[36] At

35. Unless otherwise noted, the following discussion of EEC policies is based upon Martin Holland, *The European Community and South Africa* (London: Pinter, 1988), chap. 2.

36. The ambivalent French policy of the socialist government of François Mitterrand

the end of July, European ambassadors to South Africa were temporarily recalled in preparation for a special meeting of EEC foreign ministers, where it was subsequently decided to send a diplomatic mission
to South Africa. Yet this consensus masked divisions. For example,
while Denmark officially closed consular relations, Britain insisted that
the recall of its own ambassador was merely temporary and represented
no change in its policy of dialogue.

Rejecting strong sanctions, the foreign ministers' report proposed a
package of measures aimed primarily at harmonizing existing bilateral
restrictions. It consisted of the withdrawal of military attachés from
South Africa, a ban on nuclear and military cooperation, a ban on the
sale of oil and sensitive technology, a freeze on official contacts and
international security agreements, an embargo on the European export
of arms and paramilitary equipment to South Africa, and an end to
sporting and cultural contacts. Further "positive" measures included
assistance to anti-apartheid organizations and support to the states of
the Southern African Development Coordination Conference, as well
as funds for education. Even Germany supported stronger collective
action after South Africa's announcement of an indefinite moratorium
on its loan repayments (including those owed to Germany). Hans-
Dietrich Genscher, the German foreign minister, also considered it important that the EEC not appear to lag behind the U.S. measures
adopted by President Reagan.[37] Only Britain rejected the package.

By the end of 1985, Britain had clearly lost the lead in formulating
collective European policy as other member states revised their positions on sanctions. Objecting in principle to any form of mandatory
restrictions, Britain even rejected a package of measures that it already
practiced on a voluntary basis (except for one concerning military attachés). However, bending to criticism one month later, Thatcher
adopted the new Community policy, withdrawing her military attaché
(although permitting South Africa to retain its attaché in London)
while decrying the resulting limitations on military information. Along
with these measures, member states also added provisions to the code
to dictate Community scrutiny of each country's report of compliance
with it, as well as encouraging improved relations with black trade
unions. In the area of bilateral relations, France, the Netherlands, Ire-

changed briefly to active support for sanctions during the premiership of Laurent Fabius
(1984–86); his replacement by conservative Jacques Chirac reinstated French support of
the European status quo; see Holland, *European Community*, p. 71.

37. *The Economist*, 14 September 1985, 58.

Among Females and Males in the United States, 2002 to 2012." *Alcoholism: Clinical and Experimental Research* 39 (2015): 1712–26.

Wilsnack, Richard W., and Randall Cheloha. "Women's Roles and Problem Drinking Across the Lifespan." *Social Problems* 34 (1987): 231–48.

Wilsnack, Richard W., Arlinda F. Kristjanson, Sharon C. Wilsnack, and Ross D. Crosby. "Are US Women Drinking Less (or More)? Historical and Aging Trends, 1981–2001." *Journal of Studies on Alcohol* 67 (2006): 341–48.

Wilsnack, Richard W., Nancy D. Vogeltanz, Sharon C. Wilsnack, and T. Robert Harris. "Gender Differences in Alcohol Consumption and Adverse Drinking Consequences: Cross-Cultural Patterns." *Addiction* 95 (2000): 251–65.

Wilsnack, Richard W., Sharon C. Wilsnack, and Isidore S. Obot. "Why Study Gender, Alcohol and Culture?" *Alcohol, Gender, and Drinking Problems: Perspectives from Low and Middle Income Countries. Geneva: World Health Organization* 2005 (2005): 1–25.

Wilsnack, Sharon C., and Richard W. Wilsnack. "Epidemiology of Women's Drinking." *Journal of Substance Abuse* 3 (1991): 133–57.

Woolf, Steven H., Derek A. Chapman, Jeanine M. Buchanich, Kendra J. Bobby, Emily B. Zimmerman, and Sarah M. Blackburn. "Changes in Midlife Death Rates Across Racial and Ethnic Groups in the United States: Systematic Analysis of Vital Statistics." *BMJ* 362 (2018), doi: 10.1136/bmj.k3096.

Woolf, Steven H., and Heidi Schoomaker. "Life Expectancy and Mortality Rates in the United States, 1959–2017." *JAMA* 322 (2019): 1996–2016.

World Population Review. "Blue Laws by State, 2021." June 4, 2021, https://worldpopulationreview.com/state-rankings/blue-laws-by-state.

Yao, Xiaoxin I., Michael Y. Ni, Felix Cheung, Joseph T. Wu, C. Mary Schooling, Gabriel M. Leung, and Herbert Pang. "Change in Moderate Alcohol Consumption and Quality of Life: Evidence from 2 Population-Based Cohorts." *CMAJ* 191 (2019): E753–E760.

Yuen, Wing See, Gary Chan, Raimondo Bruno, Philip Clare, Richard Mattick, Alexandra Aiken, Veronica Boland, et al. "Adolescent Alcohol Use Trajectories: Risk Factors and Adult Outcomes." *Pediatrics* 146 (2020), doi: 10.1542/peds.2020-0440.

Zipursky, Jonathan S., Nathan M. Stall, William K. Silverstein, Qing Huang, Justin Chau, Michael P. Hillmer, and Donald A. Redelmeier. "Alcohol Sales and Alcohol-Related Emergencies During the COVID-19 Pandemic." *Annals of Internal Medicine* (2021), doi:10.7326/M20-7466.

Index

land, and Denmark further restricted trade as well. Meanwhile, despite minor concessions, Britain continued to trumpet support solely for a voluntary code of business conduct.

Following the publication of the Commonwealth EPG report in July 1986, pressures mounted. A Dutch proposal to ban agricultural imports was rejected, but the Netherlands and Ireland indicated that they would nonetheless implement bilateral restrictions. The Community began to seriously consider bans on investments as well as on imports of coal, iron, steel, and gold from South Africa. With West German concurrence, however, Britain rejected these new measures.

In her capacity as the new president of the European Council, Thatcher sent Sir Geoffrey Howe (in his capacity as president of the Council of Foreign Ministers) to South Africa in July 1986 for more discussions about negotiations. This move was perceived by most critics as yet another stalling tactic, given the results of the EPG report. Even the conservative London business weekly *The Economist* referred to Thatcher's maneuvering as "attempting a diplomatic minuet in hobnail boots." Thatcher, and Germany's Kohl, rejected the Dutch interpretation that the Community would impose sanctions if Howe's mission were to fail.[38] Not surprisingly, Howe's mission did fail completely: Botha denounced it as outside interference and a threat of sanctions; the Frontline States, although willing to meet with him, dismissed the mission as useless; and Nelson Mandela, who had met twice with the EPG, refused to meet with Howe.

Any "special relationship" that Britain may have had with Botha was obviously limited. Britain lost face without improving its credibility with black South Africans. And Britain's relationship with Botha was not the only casualty of Howe's visit: Thatcher had also damaged her relationship with her foreign secretary. Before being sent to South Africa, Howe had attempted, behind the scenes, to sway Thatcher to accommodate Commonwealth views. Increasingly dissatisfied, he had nevertheless given the impression in public that Britain would adapt to Commonwealth demands for sanctions; Howe, along with other Foreign Office officials, believed Britain could not afford to be isolated on this issue. Finally, he (unsuccessfully) attempted to extract a condition from Thatcher that should his mission fail, sanctions would be considered. Tory criticism of Thatcher grew.[39]

Thatcher's marginal concessions in London set the stage for a show-

38. Ibid., 5 July 1986, 13, 44.
39. Chan, "Mrs. Thatcher," pp. 7–11.

down at the September EEC meeting. But in Europe, unlike within the Commonwealth, Britain had allies similarly arrayed against restrictions, West Germany and Portugal in particular. While accepting a partial ban on the import of iron and steel from South Africa, these allies blocked an embargo on coal imports, which would have been the most economically significant measure. The West German opinion was crucial; faced with strong opposition from the right within his ruling coalition, Chancellor Kohl refused to add coal to the list of banned imports. With Britain's objections moot owing to its Commonwealth commitment, any sanctions legislation was to be on German terms, and Kohl said that he agreed to limited sanctions only because other members supported them.[40] Although the foreign ministers tried to save face by announcing a reconsideration of the coal issue at a later date, no one took them seriously, leaving advocates of sanctions to implement bans at the bilateral level, which France and Denmark did.

Overall, in response to escalating international pressures within the Commonwealth and EEC, Britain incrementally adapted its strategic and economic relations with South Africa. This shift resulted in increasing inconsistencies: aiding the Frontline States while explicitly rejecting sanctions, and adopting restrictions while explicitly claiming to disregard international criticism. In effect, Britain adopted a policy of partial sanctions supplemented with aid to southern Africa. Not surprisingly, Britain would be the first to lift its sanctions as soon as Nelson Mandela was released from jail in February 1990.

Material interest theories cannot explain the change in British policy toward southern Africa in the mid-1980s. Since foreign-policy decision making stayed unaffected by domestic pressures, only international forces can account for the shift toward sanctions and aid to the Frontline States. British policy, therefore, offers an opportunity to gauge the extent to which affirmation of a norm of racial equality rather than security or economic costs constrained pursuit of material interests. If the costs of abrogating a norm of racial equality (by rejecting demands for sanctions) constrained the choices of a state such as Britain, which had overwhelming military and economic incentives to avoid sanctions, then norms should be even more influential in situations less conducive to explanations relying on material interests.

Furthermore, if a norm of racial equality could constrain Britain's

40. *The Economist*, 20 September 1986, 57. The Dutch backed down after Kohl telephoned the Dutch prime minister explaining his coalition's "predicament."

choices of policy toward South Africa, we have even better reason to expect that norm-enforcing sanctions would have substantial effects on a target state as well. That is, sanctions that inflict costs for violating a norm and offer rewards for adopting policies that conform with a norm should have socializing effects. By defining legitimacy, therefore, norms offer intangible benefits for community membership and identity affirmation. Sanctions provide social incentives to abide by norms.

CHAPTER EIGHT

Zimbabwe

Sanctions analysts who emphasize the material costs of opposing South Africa do not grasp the constitutive role of a norm of racial equality, especially in motivating international activism. Precisely those African states most structurally dependent on the South African economy and most damaged militarily by South African destabilization were the ones that maintained their campaign against apartheid. Neither realism nor conventional sanctions analyses can explain why African countries such as Zimbabwe absorbed the substantial costs of military antagonism and sacrificed benefits of closer economic ties for its Pan-Africanist commitment to racial equality.

In addition, regime theorists might expect the Frontline States such as Zimbabwe to join in sanctions because of incentives offered by great powers or international organizations. But rather than seeking side payments for cooperation from the United Nations, the Commonwealth, the United States, or Britain, Zimbabwe and the other Frontline States initiated calls for sanctions and pleaded for compensatory aid. African states used international institutions to strengthen a global commitment to racial equality, rather than comply with hegemonic powers. Instead of constraining their actions, the United Nations and Commonwealth actually empowered these weak states. Rather than acting as a peripheral state within southern African and international arenas, Zimbabwe took a leading role in African calls for sanctions against South Africa.

Zimbabwe's commitment to racial equality resulted from the social transformation that followed its own independence in 1980. To eluci-

date its new foreign relations with South Africa, in the first section of this chapter I examine this domestic transformation from white minority Rhodesian rule to racial equality after decolonization. From its experiences as a liberation movement in Rhodesia, the new Zimbabwean government developed a Pan-African commitment to racial equality in South Africa, and as the second section details, implementing this Pan-African regionalism in the 1980s entailed substantial economic and military costs for Zimbabwe. Its efforts at regional restructuring, I argue, demonstrate a transnational (rather than narrowly national) definition of security, threats, and interests.

Pan-African Commitment to Racial Equality

Africans in Zimbabwe have a long tradition of contesting racism both within their country and throughout the region. The national liberation movements—and future Zimbabwean government—arose out of demands for an end to white minority rule in Rhodesia. Social transformation, especially in race relations, followed independence in 1980. The activist foreign policy of the newly independent Zimbabwe thus had its roots in a Pan-Africanist commitment to racial equality established during years of exile and war.

Rejecting Minority Rule in Rhodesia

In the early 1960s, Africans objected to Britain's intention to grant independence to its federated central African colonies because of the discriminatory status quo in self-governing Rhodesia. The Zimbabwean nationalist movement radicalized, particularly after the dissolution of the Central African Federation and an increase in Rhodesian government repression that cut off legal methods of protest.[1] With their domestic activism curtailed, nationalists—allied with newly independent African states—focused on British jurisdiction for preventing independence under white minority rule.

In contrast, the Rhodesian white minority government insisted that Britain carry through on its promises of independence, trusting that

1. On the Zimbabwean nationalist movement, see Wellington Nyangoni, *African Nationalism in Zimbabwe* (Washington, D.C.: University Press of America, 1978). For an insider's view of these early years of the movement (1955–64), see Nathan Shamuyarira, *Crisis in Rhodesia* (London: Andre Deutsch, 1965). After independence, Shamuyarira became minister of information and later minister of foreign affairs.

token representation would placate the British demands for increased African political participation.[2] White Rhodesians were further affronted that the dissolution of the Central African Federation meant independence for both Zambia and Malawi yet not for the more "advanced" (and white-ruled) Rhodesia. For white Rhodesians, the issue concerned the colony's relationship with Britain, not the treatment of Africans within the territory.

Caught between these demands for independence and international pressures (especially within the Commonwealth) to improve the status of Africans, even the Conservative Macmillan government in London hesitated to end imperial oversight. While the British were not expecting immediate acceptance of a system of universal suffrage, they demanded safeguards for increased African participation. Thus their negotiations with the Rhodesians focused both on sufficient levels of African incorporation and on time frames for transitional periods.[3]

Negotiations over reform focused on the acceptability of the 1961 constitution as a basis for independence. In 1961, the British, the Rhodesians, and the Zimbabwean African People's Union (ZAPU) initially agreed upon a constitution that incorporated nominal African participation by allocating to them fifteen of the sixty-five assembly seats. Strict electoral qualifications by wealth in effect excluded all but

2. Whites frequently cited Rhodesia's historical autonomy over domestic affairs in their demands for independence. After initially being governed under the jurisdiction of the British South Africa Company, Southern Rhodesia became a self-governing colony in 1923. It was an anomaly among British colonies, neither under metropolitan control nor a Dominion. The only effective administration was local, and the powers that Britain did hold (particularly regarding the treatment of Africans) were never enforced. For example, the British government made no attempt to prevent the Land Apportionment Act of 1931, which granted the largest proportion of the best land to the whites. On white perceptions of deserved autonomy, see Margery Perham, "The Rhodesian Crisis: The Background," *International Affairs* 42 (January 1966), 1–10.

3. Macmillan's position was contained in his Five Principles (expanded to six requirements under the Wilson government): (1) unimpeded progress to majority rule, already enshrined in the 1961 constitution; (2) guarantees against any retrogressive amendment of the constitution; (3) immediate improvement in the political status of the African population; (4) progress toward ending racial discrimination; (5) British governmental satisfaction that any basis for independence should be acceptable to the people of Rhodesia as a whole; and additionally, (6) no oppression of majority by minority or minority by majority, regardless of race. On the negotiating positions, see Government of Rhodesia, Prime Minister's Department, *Relations between the Rhodesian Government and the United Kingdom Government November 1965—December 1966* (Salisbury: Government Printer, 1966), and Government of the United Kingdom, Secretary of State for Commonwealth Affairs, *Rhodesia: Documents Relating to Proposals for a Settlement* (London: HMSO, December 1966). These documents, which cover the period after November 1965, are helpful for understanding the fundamental disagreements in the early 1960s as well.

a few Africans. For the ruling white Rhodesians this minimal participation was more than enough. African leaders subsequently rejected the arrangement, because they feared that whites would alter the constitution to limit African participation further once British oversight ended.

The white Rhodesians tried various means—all short of substantial change—to mollify Britain's demands for African participation. After their election in 1962, the conservative Rhodesian Front regime took a number of approaches to justify their stand to the British, including citing the troubled Congo as a prime example of the "chaotic" consequences of African political control. Ruling white Rhodesians claimed they were protecting "Christian" civilization and values.[4]

The Rhodesian government also focused attention on chiefs as representative of African opinion (rather than explicitly nationalist groups such as ZAPU) and claimed that these chiefs unanimously supported independence. To legitimize the chieftain system, the Rhodesian Front asserted that universal suffrage was not the "traditional" way of African decision making.[5] Building upon this premise, they then suggested creating a senate composed of chiefs to complement the assembly in the 1961 system. However, such blatant exclusion of African nationalist leaders earned little international credence.

African nationalists, in the meantime, persisted in their demands for universal suffrage despite escalating governmental repression. Nationalist groups were banned almost as quickly as they were established, and their leaders detained at an equal rate. As gains from protest within the country seemed to reach their limits, many activists opted for exile. Foreign connections expanded, and nationalists increased their efforts at gaining international support for their cause, including through the newly established Organization of African Unity, the Commonwealth, and the United Nations.[6]

4. For example, see Government of Rhodesia, *Rhodesia in the Context of Africa* (Salisbury: Government Printer, 1966).

5. Government of Rhodesia, *Demand for Independence: The Domboshawa "Indaba"* (Salisbury: Government Printer, n.d. [1964?]).

6. The effectiveness of African protest was damaged by splits within the nationalist movement, most notably the formal split between ZAPU (represented by Joshua Nkomo) and the Zimbabwean African National Union (represented by N. Sithole, later by Robert Mugabe) in 1963. Disagreements centered on the degree of acceptable compromise and the balance between external and internal activism. On international aspects of the Zimbabwean nationalist movement, see Witness Mangwende, *The Organization of African Unity and the Zimbabwe Crisis: A Case Study in OAU Attempts at Collective Liberation 1963–1977* (Ph.D. diss., London School of Economics, 1979). At independence, Mangwende (a ZANU member) became minister of foreign affairs and later minister of information.

Direct pressure on the British government mounted, thanks largely to the support of independent African states. African opposition argued for the principle of no independence before majority rule, which became an international rallying cry for decolonization. As the series of negotiations between the British government and the ruling white Rhodesians stalled, the Smith regime announced its Unilateral Declaration of Independence on 11 November 1965, only to be denied international recognition. Even South Africa, which refused to alter its trading relations, refrained from formal recognition.

Immediately after UDI, Britain declared partial sanctions against Rhodesia, including bans on Rhodesian tobacco and sugar (its primary export commodities), arms transfers, and aid and credit guarantees, plus its exclusion from the sterling area and London capital markets. The UN Security Council followed suit by adopting voluntary bans on arms and oil and by urging the cessation of economic relations. One month later, Britain expanded its embargo list to include additional exports such as copper, chrome, asbestos, iron, steel, maize, and beef (for a total of 95 percent of Rhodesia's exports to Britain by value). British oil exports were also prohibited and Rhodesian assets in British banks frozen. By January 1966, virtually all exports to Rhodesia were banned. In May 1968, as resolution of the crisis remained elusive, the Security Council adopted comprehensive mandatory sanctions.[7]

African states, however, did not expect partial sanctions to bring down the Smith regime. They therefore wanted a more forceful response to UDI. If Britain were not to use military power to subdue the rebellious regime, they at least wanted comprehensive sanctions or a blockade to quickly bring the economy to a halt (presumably forcing Smith to capitulate immediately). African states declared their willingness to pay a price to reach a settlement; even Kenneth Kaunda of Zambia, the country most vulnerable to the indirect effects of sanctions against neighboring Rhodesia, advocated stronger measures and offered his country as a launching site for military action.[8]

To leaders such as Kaunda and Tanzania's Julius Nyerere, Rhodesia

7. On sanctions against Rhodesia, see William Minter and Elizabeth Schmidt, "When Sanctions Worked: The Case of Rhodesia Examined," *African Affairs* 87 (April 1988), 212. Harry R. Strack, *Sanctions: The Case of Rhodesia* (Syracuse, N.Y.: Syracuse University Press, 1978), is more comprehensive but does not extend through Zimbabwean independence.

8. Robert Good, *UDI: The International Politics of Rhodesian Rebellion* (Princeton: Princeton University Press, 1973). It was assumed Zambia would receive compensatory aid for the costs of sanctions; some aid eventually did follow.

represented part of the pervasive problem of racism in southern Africa, linked to both South African apartheid and Portuguese colonialism. Peace and prosperity in Africa as a whole required the elimination of both colonialism and racism, and Nyerere argued soon after UDI that "the Smith declaration of independence represents a counterattack by these forces, and it is in that context that Africa has reacted, and demands its defeat."[9] This Pan-African view dominated African thinking on Rhodesia and southern Africa in general.

Through the OAU's institutionalized support for liberation, the Pan-Africanists were in a position to move liberation movements toward common assumptions.[10] While reinforcing and expanding the Pan-African dimensions in the thinking of Zimbabweans, the OAU also played a crucial role in shaping—at various times both exacerbating and alleviating—the split between factions of the liberation movement. Especially in the latter half of the 1970s, their support for guerrilla war became crucial to each group's survival. The informal Frontline States alliance, acknowledged since 1974 as the formal representative of the OAU on southern African issues, maintained special access to international actors as well as to the liberation groups' leaders. Mozambique and Zambia, as staging grounds for infiltration into Rhodesia, supported the guerrilla war even further by agreeing to implement international sanctions, thus leaving Rhodesia completely dependent upon South African economic (as well as military) support.

When the combination of international sanctions and guerrilla war finally brought the Rhodesians to the bargaining table in London, the major point of controversy was whether Zimbabwe would be founded upon an institutionalized system of universal suffrage or upon one of various proposals allowing restrictions on voting rights. After contentious debates, the Lancaster House Constitution established a system based upon the principle of one person, one vote, albeit with temporary, limited safeguards for white representation in Parliament.[11] Thus with minimal modification, the Pan-Africanist view prevailed. Universal

9. Julius K. Nyerere, "Rhodesia in the Context of Southern Africa," *Foreign Affairs* 44 (April 1966), 373–74.

10. On the importance of external influence on Zimbabwean nationalists, see David Martin and Phyllis Johnson, *The Struggle for Zimbabwe: The Chimurenga War* (New York: Monthly Review Press, 1981); on the international experiences of the future prime minister, Robert Mugabe, see David Smith and Colin Simpson, *Mugabe* (Salisbury [Harare]: Pioneer Head, 1981).

11. See Jeffrey Davidow, *A Peace in Southern Africa: The Lancaster House Conference on Rhodesia, 1979* (Boulder, Colo.: Westview Press, 1984), and chap. 4 above.

suffrage replaced white minority rule, and Zimbabwe gained independence with complete international recognition.

Reconciliation in Zimbabwe

National elections (under British jurisdiction and Commonwealth supervision) put the Zimbabwean African National Union, the most radical of the liberation groups, into power upon independence 18 April 1980. Clearly ZANU had succeeded in mobilizing the majority of Africans behind its image as the victors in the guerrilla war. Zimbabweans expected equal opportunities and compensation for past discrimination. Accordingly, the political agenda of the new Zimbabwean regime differed substantially from the previous Rhodesian one.

Avowedly marxist, Prime Minister Robert Mugabe raised expectations for dramatic economic redistribution and political reorganization. Whites dreaded the consequences of majority rule. Although many stayed, almost half resettled in South Africa, Britain, and Australia. Their fears, however, soon seemed unwarranted, as the new regime made few radical changes. Mugabe quickly earned a reputation as a pragmatist. Constitutional provisions further restricted the new regime, requiring payment in hard currency for land. Parliamentary institutions, parastatal control of crucial sectors of the economy, and the extensive security establishment all remained intact, although blacks did replace many whites within them.

Mugabe also decided to limit nationalization in order to retain skilled whites (to avoid repeating Mozambique's experience with white flight). Encouraging whites to remain, however, also ensured their continued control of the economy. Within these constraints and with the help of foreign-trained technocrats in the economic ministries, the government established a new working relationship with those whites in charge of the country's agricultural and industrial sectors.[12] This was one consequence of Mugabe's "reconciliation" policy. Concessions to whites, he argued, were necessary to establish stability in a war-torn country.

This reconciliation policy eased the transition to majority rule, but tensions remained between government and business. Hoping to downplay conflict, the government appeased the private sector by limiting economic restructuring, and a similar commitment from the busi-

12. On these new sectoral relationships, see Jeffrey Herbst, *State Politics in Zimbabwe* (Berkeley: University of California Press, 1990).

ness community kept its criticisms of government policy to a minimum. Muted criticism on both sides characterized their new working relationship, and this moderation carried over to racial dynamics as well. Business leaders, and most whites, distanced themselves from conservative racism and publicly conformed to new expectations of racial equality. Dissent, if expressed at all, remained private.

Within this new social and political context, Zimbabweans debated their new relationship with South Africa. The government's domestic policies reflected a commitment to reconciliation and the evolution of a working relationship with the business community, leaving foreign relations as the one area where the new government could clearly break with the Rhodesian legacy. Although limited by structural economic dependence on South Africa (the result of prolonged international sanctions and the Rhodesians' need for support from its southern neighbor), Zimbabwe sought to reduce those ties and to expand its diplomatic contacts around the world. In contrast to Rhodesia's isolation, Zimbabwe joined the United Nations, the Organization of African Unity, the Commonwealth, the Non-Aligned Movement, and other international organizations. Signaling its stance against apartheid, it became the newest member of the Frontline States alliance and a founding member of the Southern African Development Coordination Conference, both exemplary manifestations of Pan-Africanist perspectives on southern Africa.

TRANSNATIONAL VERSUS NATIONAL INTERESTS

In pursuit of a broad goal of nonracialism consistent with his visions of both Zimbabwean development and progress in international affairs, Mugabe persistently condemned South Africa's apartheid and its increasingly aggressive policy of destabilization. In contrast to the Rhodesian regime, his definition of security presumed a commitment to racial equality. In practice, tensions between Pan-African transnational interests and national interests (and advocates of each) produced a mixture of regional policies, ranging from military involvement in Mozambique to the protection of national economic prosperity.

New Definitions of Security

Unlike Ian Smith, Robert Mugabe viewed South Africa as a fundamental threat to the survival of his country and regime, as evident in the debates over renewal of the state of emergency in the House of Assembly (first in the Rhodesian and later in the Zimbabwean parliament). Whereas the Smith regime consistently justified the emergency decree by pointing to the threat of "communist" insurgents funded by outside powers (including the alleged collusion of Western powers), Prime Minister Mugabe cited "racist" South Africa's efforts to undermine the regime through insurgency and destabilization. In both cases the nature of the threat was the same: outsiders based in neighboring countries propagating an ideology repulsive to the regime. Only the content of that ideology differed.[13]

Consequently, the two regimes pursued contrasting relationships with South Africa. The Rhodesian Front had relied on South Africa for both economic and military aid as international sanctions and the guerrilla war escalated, but the new ZANU government viewed that economic dependence as a structural impediment to their development plans and a source of political weakness. To Mugabe, South African racism was the underlying cause of the regional tensions and instabilities that diverted Zimbabwean resources from development to defense. Consequently, one of the immediate goals of the new regime was to alter the regional economic balance so as to reduce South African control. It pursued this aim in part by joining SADCC, the regional development organization.

The Zimbabwean regime viewed South Africa as an equally formidable threat to its fundamental domestic goals. Not only did apartheid symbolize the antithesis of the new Zimbabwean domestic order based on racial equality, but the policies of the South African regime also presented an immediate threat to the new regime's domestic stability and legitimacy. Certainly the South African government had not been happy that ZANU, rather than one of its more moderate rivals, had come to power in 1980. Mugabe's pragmatic socialism threatened the South African leaders' vehement anticommunism, and his policy of domestic reconciliation set the stage for the "Zimbabwe model"—the viable example of coexistence of black and white under African majority rule—which shook the philosophical foundations of apartheid.[14] South

13. First instituted by the Rhodesian Front just days before UDI, the state of emergency remained in effect throughout Rhodesian rule and was subsequently renewed by the Zimbabwean regime. The state-of-emergency legislation, which had always been framed in terms of threats to national security, clearly contrasts the Rhodesian and Zimbabwean perspectives; see House of Assembly, *Parliamentary Debates* (Government Printer, serial). It was finally lifted in July 1990.

14. According to apartheid philosophy, coexistence was not possible without the de-

African efforts to subvert Mugabe's policy of reconciliation took a number of forms, including spying and sabotage, as well as support for anti-ZANU dissidents in the western part of the country.

Mugabe's policies frustrated South African regional plans as well. Zimbabwe's alignment with the Frontline States and its participation in the founding of SADCC in 1980 ended South African hopes of regional economic domination through their Constellation of Southern African States policy, and with it any hopes of expanded influence in other areas of Africa. As a result, South Africa's efforts at regional destabilization intensified. Tactics included sabotage and economic non-cooperation with an overshadowing threat of further military action. Such implicit and explicit threats increased as Mugabe took on a more vocal role internationally in support of comprehensive mandatory sanctions.

As independence brought Zimbabwe international recognition for its policy of reconciliation and its relatively fruitful development efforts, Mugabe increasingly viewed the country's success in creating a prosperous nonracial society as one of the most important causes of South African attempts to undermine his government. Consequently he considered the costs of policies such as economic sanctions against South Africa to be short-term necessities in the face of a fundamental threat to the new Zimbabwean society. Conversely, the regime anticipated that elimination of apartheid would lead to the end of destabilization, which was a precondition for any peace at home or in the region.

Initially, Mugabe's stance against South Africa and his emphasis on international nonalignment were uncontroversial; indeed, these policies won prestige for a country that had previously, as Rhodesia, had been shunned in international affairs. Domestic debates heated up as the international movement for sanctions gained momentum in 1985, but full-fledged controversy erupted only upon Mugabe's announcement in August 1986 that Zimbabwe would implement the Commonwealth package of partial sanctions. None of his critics publicly questioned the importance of eliminating apartheid, but many questioned the wisdom of sanctions, given the repercussions for the domestic economy.

Zimbabweans contested the type of sanctions policy but not the goal. Most debates centered on the potential costs of reducing ties with South Africa. Even those most skeptical of the regime—the business community—did not publicly reject the importance of promoting ra-

struction of white racial and cultural identity. For more on the "Zimbabwe model," see *Zimbabwe's Prospects*, ed. Colin Stoneman (London: Macmillan, 1988).

cial equality. Ensuing public debates also focused on complementary trade and transport development policies. Differing views of transnational and national interests resulted in contending perspectives on the acceptable costs of opposing South African apartheid.

Weighing the Costs of Sanctions

Intense debate over sanctions beginning in 1985 focused on Zimbabwe's economic dependence on South Africa. Concentrating particularly on the transport routes that affected almost all import and export traffic, competing estimates of the domestic, regional, and global costs were offered. The government emphasized the current costs of destabilization; its critics claimed that sanctions against South Africa would lead to the total collapse of the Zimbabwean economy. The lack of irrefutable economic analysis fueled the political nature of this debate.

Rather than denying that costs would be involved, Mugabe stressed the country's need to bear the burden and overcome economic difficulties. Along with the other Frontline leaders, he pursued international sources of compensatory aid in 1985 and 1986. Some Western aid was forthcoming, particularly for SADCC, but support more explicitly aimed at facilitating the implementation of sanctions was less readily available. Even countries that had been crucial in the recent shift to consensus on sanctions (specifically Australia and Canada) were against these southern African states' attempting sanctions and consequently were not forthcoming with pledges of financial assistance.[15]

Although the countries most capable of significant support, including the United States and members of the European Community, were unwilling to make such promises, various non-Western countries did come forward to help. Most outspoken were members of the Commonwealth and of the OAU and the Non-Aligned Movement, notably India and Nigeria. The Non-Aligned Movement (primarily through India) set up a liberation support fund designed to give financial assistance to the Frontline States.[16] Nigeria also offered substantial financial backing for this project, in addition to a similar effort through the OAU.[17]

15. Their positions changed somewhat by 1987, when Commonwealth member states, including Britain, offered more aid, but this was after the height of debates in Zimbabwe. See chaps. 4 and 7 above.

16. The Non-Aligned Movement announced a Fund against South Africa after its August–September 1986 summit meeting in Harare; see *The Herald* (Harare), 10 September 1986.

17. The government also heavily publicized the establishment (on 21 March 1986) of

Not surprisingly, the Zimbabwean government publicized pledges of support while downplaying more ambivalent responses. Mugabe simultaneously attempted to discredit domestic opponents of his policy, charging critics with "defeatism" for overestimating costs and undervaluing the goal of defeating apartheid. He also excoriated his critics for ignoring his government's persistent suggestions since independence that businesses should develop new markets that would free them from reliance on South Africa.[18]

The business community remained vulnerable to accusations of undue sympathy for white-ruled South Africa. For example, in a late October 1985 public television broadcast, the president of the Confederation of Zimbabwean Industries, John Mkusi, declared that sanctions would cause the total collapse of the Zimbabwean economy within months. In response, the progovernment press echoed Mugabe's earlier condemnation, claiming that "obviously our capitalists . . . brought up in the comfort of a way of life derived from the exploitation of others . . . are cool and detached about [apartheid] until their comfort may be affected. . . . In the end the advice [about damage to the Zimbabwean economy] reveals itself for what it is: a call to surrender and collaborate with the unrepentant oppressors of the black people of South Africa." Nor were the government and press the only critics of the CZI president; some other members of the CZI itself dissociated themselves from his comments.[19]

Clarifying his comments and leaks from a highly confidential CZI report on the effects of sanctions, Mkusi complained in early November that his original statement, which emphasized the importance of repairing Mozambican trade routes, had been unfairly overshadowed by his remarks on sanctions. His attempt to downplay disagreement with the government ran into further difficulties as rumors circulated that the CZI had also attempted to influence Prime Minister Mugabe's position at the concurrent Commonwealth summit meeting in Nassau. The press speculated about whose interests the CZI was serving. The CZI and other organizations needed to be brought in line with the aspirations of the black majority, the major Harare daily *The Herald*

---

a domestic liberation support fund to compensate workers unemployed as a result of sanctions; see *The Herald,* 24 September 1986.

18. Ibid., 23 October 1985.

19. Ibid., 22 October, 29 October, and 7 November 1985. Some of these members represented parastatal corporations. The division within CZI was not along racial lines; John Mkusi was black, as were the other four top officials who resigned.

claimed, not solely out of moral obligation but for reasons of self-inter-est as well.[20]

In response to escalating criticisms and internal divisions, the CZI then took out a full-page advertisement in *The Herald* (on 12 November 1985) listing twenty-two points of clarification of its position. Never, the ad proclaimed, had the CZI said that the Zimbabwean government should not campaign for sanctions; indeed, the organization was not seeking involvement in such a political issue but rather pointing out risks and consequences so as to prepare the economy to sustain sanc-tions. Again, "urgent" development of alternative trade routes was championed. The ad smoothed over any conflict with the government and denied that the black president of the organization had been used in order to say what others (presumably whites) felt unable to say. The CZI was, it reasserted, defending the broad interests of its members and the "Nation" (which it identified with economic independence). Nor was it attempting to influence government policy. Finally, the ad reaffirmed the organization's unequivocal opposition to apartheid and its record of support for the Zimbabwean government.

Also in the days following the initial controversy, *The Financial Gazette* attempted to articulate a position between Mkusi's reported stance and that of the government press. The independent weekly confirmed the business community's public moderation. On moral grounds, its edi-torial announced, "the country must condemn the South African politi-cal system and encourage change." Yet Mkusi's concern about eco-nomic collapse was correct, it added, leading to the conclusion that a "less confrontational" policy was essential.[21] Two months later the paper pragmatically argued that Zimbabwe "must be prepared to endure" the indirect economic damage caused by of international (particularly Commonwealth) sanctions and should even implement low-cost sanc-tions of its own; implementation, however, should be gradual, to allow time for developing alternative trade routes.[22]

Attempting to discredit the persistent concern over costs expressed by the CZI and echoed by *The Financial Gazette*, *The Herald* (on 28 No-vember 1985) quoted the highly respected minister of finance, Ber-nard Chidzero, as saying that sanctions would not bring economic col-lapse, although there would be some shortages and hardships (which required contingency plans and international support). On an upbeat

20. Ibid., 7 November 1985.
21. *The Financial Gazette* (Harare), 25 October 1985.
22. Ibid., 6 December 1985.

note, he added that foreign investment could shift from South Africa to Zimbabwe. A few days later Chidzero appeared on television reiterating that Zimbabwe would survive sanctions given the healthy state of the economy, so support for them was justifiable.[23]

Business and government continued to disagree over the costs of sanctions, but their overriding consensus on the long-term goal of economic independence did produce agreement on a contingency plan for sanctions: the development of alternative trading routes through Mozambique. Previously the government had spent few resources developing alternatives. Now the newly created Beira Corridor Group, chaired by Denis Norman, was to coordinate international fund-raising and planning for the rehabilitation of railways between Mutare, in the northwest of Zimbabwe, and Beira, the closest Mozambican port.[24]

Cooperation on the Beira Corridor reinforced the moderate relationship between business and government. The government's attempts to silence business criticism culminated in the announcement by the CZI in July 1986 that it now supported comprehensive sanctions against South Africa; apartheid was inimical to economic progress, they declared.[25] Furthermore, after the South African bombing of ANC offices in Harare in May 1986, both business and government stepped up their criticism of the South Africa regime. Fear of South African retaliation grew during succeeding months, particularly as the international drive for sanctions advanced.[26] Mugabe became even more convinced

23. *The Herald*, 2 December 1985. *The Financial Gazette* (29 November 1985) printed Chidzero's speech, including his comment, "This is not to say that the economy would collapse but rather that it would function at a reduced rate, generating unemployment, shortage of goods, and general hardship." *The Herald* emphasized his statement that investment might shift from South Africa, which Chidzero qualified by adding that, alternatively, the whole region could become unstable, leading to increased disinvestment all around. The effects of sanctions were contingent, he added, on the political, economic, and financial response of the international community.

24. Norman, a prominent white Zimbabwean, had been minister of agriculture in Mugabe's first cabinet. Colonial Rhodesia had used these alternative routes until Mozambican independence and imposition of sanctions in 1975; only in the late 1970s did transport become totally dependent on South African ports.

25. *The Herald*, 4 July 1986. An editorial on 6 July 1986 in *The Sunday Mail* (the Sunday edition of the *Herald*), however, cast doubt on the sincerity of this CZI declaration. Rumors also circulated that privately none of the members supported sanctions. In addition, *The Financial Gazette* (11 July 1986) reported objections from CZI members over the voting procedures used on the proposal.

26. Such fears culminated in the death of Samora Machel in a plane crash in South African territory. South Africa's culpability was widely assumed, though never proven. As the military threat from South Africa rose, Mugabe reiterated his calls for a Pan-African

of the need for sanctions against South Africa and reiterated that his country could not be secure without the elimination of apartheid. Even *The Financial Gazette* stated (on 23 May 1986) that the Pretoria regime and its struggle to retain power were the source of unrest, instability, and violence in the whole southern African region.

Reaffirming his opposition to South Africa, Mugabe became even more active on behalf of sanctions both abroad and at home. The focus on the Beira Corridor had helped to dispel domestic criticism of the government's stand on sanctions, but controversy flared anew. Serious discussion of the Commonwealth package, including highly visible measures such as a ban on air links, followed the London minisummit in early August 1986. Mugabe announced his intention of adopting Commonwealth measures (and indicated that he would abide by even more stringent ones if agreed to at the upcoming Non-Aligned summit) but gave no formal directive. Implementation, he said, would most likely begin by the end of 1986—the Commonwealth had tentatively settled on November—while work on alternative trade routes proceeded as quickly as possible. He assured Zimbabweans that although they would suffer, the country would survive.[27] In support of Mugabe's stand, *The Herald* wrote (on 9 August 1986), "To those who say the move is tantamount to suicide, we can only say that the way things are going we are being slowly strangled anyway."

The nature of criticism of Mugabe's stand on sanctions had now shifted: business was no longer his major detractor. Just prior to the Commonwealth minisummit, on 18 July 1986 *The Financial Gazette* declared its support for coordinated international pressures because "the futility of dialogue with the South African government without accompanying pressure has been demonstrated since the last Commonwealth conference. A year has been wasted and more lives lost." It was the nature of these measures, however, that needed to be decided; Secretary-General Ramphal's call for a structured set of Commonwealth compromise measures was lauded. Their effectiveness would depend on how they were applied and by whom. Costs were still under debate, but by September 1986 the principle of sanctions had been accepted. This

---

army, but he received insufficient support. There were also proposals at the Non-Aligned summit a few months later to establish a military force, but these, too, lacked substantial support. See Stephen Chan, "Foreign Policies in Southern Africa: The History of an Epoch, 1978–88," in his edited *Exporting Apartheid: Foreign Policies in Southern Africa 1978–1988* (New York: St. Martin's, 1990), pp. 84–85.

27. *The Herald,* 9 August 1986.

shift in opinion coincided with wide-ranging international support for sanctions. With the exception of Britain, the Commonwealth countries agreed to partial sanctions in August 1986; the European Community passed similar measures in September; and the United States adopted more stringent sanctions in October.

Nonetheless, Prime Minister Mugabe repeatedly postponed Zimbabwe's implementation of the Commonwealth measures. Having proclaimed his intention to cut off trade with South Africa, he explained that planning and preparation continued. Finally, as the international momentum for sanctions stalled, he let the matter drop without actually reversing himself. Ironically, after having publicly overcome opposition from the business community, and despite his personal commitment to implementation, Mugabe was apparently dissuaded from following through on these bilateral sanctions by key cabinet advisors who warned of both economic and military consequences.[28]

The decision to postpone restrictions was based not merely on cost but on disagreements over which costs were acceptable. Zimbabwe was already bearing substantial costs for developing the Beira Corridor and maintaining a military force in Mozambique, which protected the rail and pipelines from sabotage by the rebel Mozambique National Resistance. Since June 1985, the Zimbabwean government (along with Tanzania) had been providing army protection for the Beira Corridor and additional support to the Mozambican army to combat these Renamo guerrillas. Troop levels escalated as the needs for protection expanded. Having based his own guerrilla movement in Mozambique, Mugabe felt personal as well as Pan-African obligations to support Machel's government against the South African–supported resistance movement. Thus Zimbabwe maintained defense expenditures near Rhodesian wartime levels.[29]

In contrast to military involvement in Mozambique, which was pri-

28. The actual cabinet discussions are notoriously difficult to document, with most reporting based on rumors. However, fairly consistent reports claim that Mugabe was restrained by his cabinet, particularly after apparent threats of military retaliation from South Africa; see esp. Chan, "Foreign Policies," p. 82. There was also rumored to be grumbling among key cabinet members that Mugabe had unadvisedly changed policy in declaring his intention to implement bilateral restrictions; see *Africa Confidential* 27 (1986), 7.

29. During the 1980s, Zimbabwean defense expenditures ranged between 12 and 15 percent of the total budget. Before the escalation of the guerrilla war, Rhodesian expenditures were at 8 percent, rising to 18 percent in 1979. These figures are based on statistics in *Report of the Comptroller and Auditor-General* (Government Printer, Salisbury/Harare, annual). On military involvement in Mozambique, also see chap. 5 above.

marily the prime minister's (uncontested) decision, sanctions had become more than a foreign policy issue. They therefore were of concern beyond the traditional foreign policy–making establishment. Factionalism between populists and technocrats within the ruling ZANU party, a split that was reproduced within the cabinet, became unusually salient among foreign-policy makers.[30] The populists were calling for sanctions, but the technocrats cautioned restraint. Mugabe could not dismiss the economic concerns of his cabinet with the same tactics he had used with the business community; party members could not be accused of undue sympathy for racists in South Africa.

This split in the cabinet precluded escalating sanctions. It also produced a compromise consisting of strong support for a combination of economic and military involvement in Mozambique. The populist faction placed greater importance on the survival of the Mozambican regime, and the technocrats accepted the budget increases. Although Mugabe was unable to discredit the concerns of the technocrat faction, the populist ideals at the foundation of the party's political agenda—including its Pan-Africanist commitment to racial equality—continued to shape foreign policy. Vociferous public debate over the costs and benefits of anti-apartheid sanctions were part of a broader process of defining threats and national interests in the new state.

Zimbabwe's promotion of international sanctions and its commitment to economic restructuring in southern Africa contradicts conventional sanctions analysts, who would predict economic incentives and military threats to far outweigh any commitment to a norm of racial equality. Zimbabwe's very contemplation of economic sanctions against South Africa illustrates that racial equality—rather than simply military and economic interests—mattered. Mugabe's personal commitment to racial equality and the support of the populist faction within his party led to Zimbabwean advocacy of Commonwealth sanctions in 1986, even though it postponed implementation because alternative trade routes had yet to be secured. As a result of accommodation between Pan-Africanists and economic nationalists, Zimbabwe also pursued complementary—and costly—regional policies; investing in regional political and economic restructuring required armed protection for

---

30. I borrow this distinction between populists and technocrats from Ronald T. Libby, *Economic Power in Southern Africa* (Princeton: Princeton University Press, 1987), who cites factionalism in economic policy making. There are no comparable published analyses of the politics of foreign-policy decision making.

the transport and pipeline routes through Mozambique. A focus on material costs especially overlooks Zimbabwe's fears of South Africa's destabilization.

Consequently social costs and benefits need to be incorporated into any assessment of African foreign policies and, by extension, into our assessments of strength and weakness. South Africa's advocacy of white superiority ultimately undermined its security and ability to control regional relations, despite its overwhelming objective military and economic capabilities, because apartheid undermined Zimbabwe's goal of a domestic society based on racial equality. Conflicts between advocates of racial superiority and racial equality defined threats, security, and interests in social terms. Africans calculated costs and benefits in ways that transcended territorial state boundaries and incorporated a continental commitment to racial equality. Thus regional relations and Zimbabwean foreign policy illustrate the implications of social power and transnational commitments.

Part IV

IMPLICATIONS

CHAPTER NINE

Sanctions and South African Reform

When in 1991 the South African government initiated legal reforms that removed the formal pillars of apartheid, it fulfilled international demands for the elimination of apartheid, and consequently most sanctions were lifted. International observers who were previously skeptical of the effectiveness of sanctions now proclaimed the success of international pressures for reform. But most analysts of sanctions focus on tactical shifts in foreign policy rather than link international sanctions to domestic structures such as a constitutional system of racial segregation.[1] Thus they cannot explain why the South African government would transform its domestic institutions in response to international demands. The demise of apartheid, culminating in universal-suffrage elections in April 1994, challenges the conventional skepticism about sanctions and demonstrates the theoretical and practical implications of taking norms seriously.

Building on the theoretical arguments and empirical lessons of the preceding chapters, I now turn to the ways in which norm-enforcing sanctions might have affected reform in South Africa. As I have already illustrated, conventional sanctions analysts generally follow realist assumptions. In a realist context, the broad range of reactions to South African domestic racial discrimination is surprising. Particularly strik-

1. For example, in response to international condemnation of apartheid, South Africa has at various times attempted to improve its foreign relations with other African states through (unsuccessful) "detente" initiatives. See James Barber and John Barratt, *South Africa's Foreign Policy: The Search for Status and Security, 1945–1988* (Cambridge: Cambridge University Press, 1990), and chap. 5 above.

ing are the efforts of African states to challenge South Africa not only within international organizations as the United Nations but also regionally, through the Organization of African Unity, despite almost overwhelming economic and military costs. Even the more nuanced regime theory analyses underestimate the effectiveness of anti-apartheid activists. Notably, multilateral cooperation within the Commonwealth produced collective sanctions against South Africa, British opposition notwithstanding. Finally, challenging both realist and regime perspectives that define power in terms of material capabilities, these activists provoked U.S. congressional sanctions despite the objections of a popular president. In sum, the experiences of transnational anti-apartheid activists demonstrated the importance of legitimation processes and social incentives, contradicting the tenets of theorists whose scope is limited to coercion and material capabilities.

From this emphasis on socialization, I argue that South Africa's elimination of apartheid was indeed partially a response to global—and not solely domestic—pressures. I discuss three ways in which international pressures influenced South African domestic reform in the following analysis: first, the strategic effects of sanctions on the South Africa's military and economic capabilities, as seen by realists; then, the external incentives for government-instigated reforms, according to regime theory; and third, the effects of international legitimation on various domestic groups, with a stress on interpretive arguments. My conclusion is that reform through inducement corresponds to neoliberal market-power explanations of the relationship between norms and behavior, and legitimation corresponds to interpretive social-power explanations. Both these aspects of international pressure on South Africa reinforce my general claim that international relations theorists and sanctions analysts in particular must move beyond the realist focus on coercive power and material interests.

COERCION EFFECTS

For most conventional critics, sanctions lack the power to coerce—in contrast to military means—because they are rarely capable of inflicting high costs on the target state.[2] Yet ample empirical evidence, using

2. Rhodesia is the classic example. Johan Galtung even claims that sanctions can be counterproductive by generating new elites whose interests lie in maintaining interna-

consistent criteria, demonstrates that sanctions can be effective in altering the behavior of target states.[3] Thus under certain circumstances, sanctions do succeed in compelling and deterring, as strategic analysts would argue. But because of South Africa's general resistance to external threats, it earned a reputation as an isolationist "laager" state reminiscent of the Afrikaner settlers' circling their wagons against attack.[4] Therefore, while the eventual abolition of apartheid supports these optimistic assessments of the utility of sanctions, we have little reason to conclude that South African reform resulted simply from threats and coercion.

Moving beyond this narrow behavioral approach, some analysts working within a realist framework also focus on the effects of sanctions on military capabilities. Still most concerned with coercive power, these analysts nonetheless acknowledge that international pressures can alter internal—structural—characteristics of a state. Adding an economic component to military considerations, these strategic analysts suggest the use of sanctions in economic warfare. Sanctions may undermine the target state's defense by damaging its economy or by increasing the opportunity costs of military procurement. Sanctions may also deprive the target state of crucial technology.[5]

Sophisticated strategic perspectives consequently emphasize that arms embargoes changed South Africa's military capabilities in the costly direction of import substitution. But South Africa remained vulnerable because it still secretly imported its most sophisticated equip-

---

tional isolation; see his "On the Effects of International Economic Sanctions," *World Politics* 19 (April 1967), 378–416. Most studies of the South African case were published before the peak of reforms in 1990–91 and depicted sanctions as ineffective because they did not profoundly damage the South African economy.

3. The broadest empirical study of sanctions is Gary Clyde Hufbauer, Jeffrey J. Schott, and Kimberly Ann Elliott, *Economic Sanctions Reconsidered: History and Current Policy*, 2d ed. (Washington, D.C.: Institute for International Economics, 1990). The authors measure effectiveness in terms of the target state's response, considering both the extent to which the policy outcome sought by the sender country was in fact achieved and the contribution made by the sanctions. Because of the subjectivity of their evaluations (which they acknowledge), the study's value is in its consistency across cases.

4. Analysts offer a range of explanations for South Africa's isolationism. See variously Barber and Barrett, *South African Foreign Policy;* Deon Geldenhuys, *The Diplomacy of Isolation: South African Foreign Policy Making* (New York: St. Martin's, 1984); and contributions in *Exporting Apartheid: Foreign Policies in Southern Africa 1978–1988*, ed. Stephen Chan (New York: St. Martin's, 1990).

5. See especially Michael Mastanduno, *Economic Containment: CoCom and the Politics of East-West Trade* (Ithaca: Cornell University Press, 1992), and Bruce W. Jentleson, *Pipeline Politics: The Complex Political Economy of East-West Energy* (Ithaca: Cornell University Press, 1986).

ment from European sources. Economic sanctions also led it to develop strategies for import substitution, including coal-to-oil processing capabilities. Again, South Africa was still economically vulnerable because it needed to import capital to maintain economic growth in the medium and long term.[6] Thus South Africa stayed structurally vulnerable to global pressures despite its isolationist behavior, and its leaders may have responded to international sanctions because of increasing internal weakness. Indeed, South Africa's negotiated settlement of Namibian independence fits this type of argument.

However, even a strategic capabilities argument is based on the assumption that states adapt to preserve their national strategic (and aggregate economic) interests. But since the South African government defined white minority rule as essential to national survival, strategic perspectives still fail to explain why the National Party would peacefully negotiate itself out of power. More complicated assessments of costs, benefits, and risks presumably challenged the Afrikaners' belief that control of the state ensured their survival. In other words, a traditional focus on the consequences of sanctions for foreign policy ignores the stated goal of international pressures against South Africa: domestic transformation. Thus we need theoretical perspectives that disaggregate the state, economically and politically.

INCENTIVE EFFECTS

Since conventional international relations perspectives take the state to be a unitary, rational actor, most sanctions studies cannot elucidate the domestic implications of structural change. The general relationship between economic variables and political processes and institutions is underspecified. Even discussions of the South Africa case mostly emphasize the economic effects of economic measures and neglect other significant political aspects of international sanctions.[7] In

6. For a general overview of the capability effects of international sanctions, see Robert M. Price, *The Apartheid State in Crisis: Political Transformation in South Africa 1975–1990* (New York: Oxford University Press, 1991), chap. 7. I thank Neta Crawford for drawing my attention to the capability argument.

7. For an example in the South African case, see Charles M. Becker, "Economic Sanctions against South Africa," *World Politics* 39 (January 1987), 147–73. Although unusually explicit about this political connection, William H. Kaempfer and Anton D. Lowenberg rely on general "economic hardship" as the source of "political pressure." What distinguishes their argument from the realists', however, is the emphasis on the influ-

addition, analyses of political reform in South Africa focus on the balance of power between domestic actors (primarily the National Party, the African National Congress, and the Zulu-based Inkatha Freedom Party) while minimizing institutional and international factors.[8] Thus we need to understand how these external threats and structural changes might have convinced South African leaders to institute a domestic political system based on a norm of racial equality.

As our analyses of U.S., British, and Zimbabwean foreign policies have demonstrated, global norms can influence the definition of state interests and policy choices through a variety of transmission mechanisms, even in the most centralized decision-making institutions. One mechanism is the alteration of external costs and benefits, in terms of both economic and social incentives. International memberships and diplomatic sanctions, for example, might influence the target state's behavior even in the absence of substantial economic costs. As the British case best demonstrates, external costs and benefits are measured in social as well as economic and military terms. Thus international pressures can create incentives far beyond the strictly economic.

Various aspects of South African reform indicate that political and economic sanctions promoted a norm of racial equality within South Africa. But since incorporation of a global norm of racial equality has diverse indicators that reflect broad social and individual attitudes (just the reverse of apartheid's systematic promotion of racial segregation throughout South Africa's political, economic, and social structures), ideally, we would want to identify the extent to which a norm gets incorporated throughout a country's social, political, and economic structures, as well as into individuals' psyches. As a first step in that direction, let us focus here on the requirements for political reform listed within international sanctions packages (such as the Commonwealth measures and the U.S. Comprehensive Anti-Apartheid Act). These conditions delineated the behavioral response from the South African gov-

---

ence of interest groups within the target state; see *International Economic Sanctions: A Public Choice Perspective* (Boulder, Colo.: Westview Press, 1992), p. 11.

8. That interest-group analyses underestimate political institutions is particularly problematic since groups within South Africa were fighting specifically over alternative post-apartheid constitutional arrangements. See Donald L. Horowitz, *A Democratic South Africa? Constitutional Engineering in a Divided Society* (Berkeley: University of California Press, 1991). Few analyses of domestic South African politics recognize an international dimension; noteworthy exceptions are Stanley Greenberg, "Economic Growth and Political Change: The South African Case," *Journal of Modern African Studies* 19 (December 1981), 667–704; Price, *Apartheid State*; and Anthony W. Marx, *Lessons of Struggle: South African Internal Opposition, 1960–1990* (New York: Oxford University Press, 1992).

ernment that its critics would consider sufficient evidence of compliance with the norm.

South Africa's international opponents broadly claimed to strive for the elimination of apartheid, and debates over sanctions produced specific criteria for progress toward racial equality. This issue of criteria for compliance is one important aspect of the external debates over sanctions in the sender countries and multilateral institutions that frequently has been ignored or underestimated. These international agreements can be distilled into five specific government-initiated reforms that most international actors considered necessary, and usually sufficient, to allow the lifting of those restrictions. The South African government was called upon to (1) repeal the state of emergency; (2) release all political prisoners; (3) unban the ANC and other political parties; (4) eliminate apartheid laws; and (5) enter into negotiations for a new political system.[9]

It is against these five conditions that an initial evaluation of sanctions against South Africa ought to be made. While not conclusive proof of the importance of sanctions, a brief survey of the progression of South African post-1989 government-sponsored reforms—which followed these five criteria with considerable accuracy—indicates a plausible relationship between international sanctions and reform.

South African president F. W. de Klerk came to power at the end of 1989 amid growing domestic and international pressure for reform. International sanctions were an important component of that pressure, as indicated by the timing and order of de Klerk's reforms, as well as by the justifications he offered for his policies. Although not his first, perhaps the most important of de Klerk's reforms was the release of Nelson Mandela on 12 February 1990. Gaining credibility by freeing the world's most famous political prisoner (in addition to various others), de Klerk also supported this largely symbolic gesture with more substantial political reforms, notably by unbanning the ANC, as well as other previously outlawed and arguably more radical organizations, including the Pan-African Congress and the South African Communist Party, on 2 February 1990. A third substantial reform was de Klerk's repeal of the national state of emergency that had been im-

9. Wording and emphasis differed marginally among agreements but show surprising consistency given the difficulty of international agreement in general. Some actors called for more concrete evidence of a transition to majority rule (such as one-person, one-vote elections, for example); the measures listed here represent the more conservative interpretation of reform.

posed in 1986 at the height of domestic unrest; despite domestic conservative pressure he refused to reimpose it in the face of continuing unrest in the townships. In a related move, de Klerk also lifted some of the most repressive features of the Internal Security Act of 1982 (such as detention without trial) that the government had used to restrict anti-apartheid activities. Opening up the political process and releasing political prisoners, de Klerk quickly fulfilled three of the five international conditions.[10]

De Klerk's repeal of the legal pillars of apartheid, fulfilling a fourth condition, progressed in stages and involved more complex political maneuvering. In a preliminary measure, parliament repealed the Separate Amenities Act in June 1990, lifting racial segregation in public areas such as parks and restrooms. More substantial legislative action on 5 June 1991 included the repeal of both the Group Areas Act, which classified residential areas according to racial criteria, and the Land Acts, which did the same for ownership areas (thus underpinning the homeland system as well as white ownership of 87 percent of South African territory). Furthermore, on 17 June 1991, the parliament repealed the Population Registration Act, which defined the different racial classifications underlying all other apartheid legislation. Indeed, de Klerk explicitly defended his reforms on the grounds that apartheid restrictions were "evidently unjust, in conflict with the Christian values to which we profess to aspire, *contrary to internationally acceptable norms,* and a certain recipe for revolt, revolution, and civil war" (emphasis added).[11]

Finally, to convince international sanctioners that his government was sincerely pursuing political reform, de Klerk needed to undertake negotiations with opposition representatives—"talks about talks"—that would go beyond the earlier, informal (and officially secret) talks that had taken place between the government and imprisoned leaders such as Mandela. Entering into formal talks with the ANC by May 1991, de Klerk convinced most international governments that his intentions for

10. Controversy persisted, however, over whether the South African government had released all political prisoners. Opposition movements charged that many remained incarcerated for political crimes; the government denied the claim. In U.S. debates over the repeal of sanctions, President Bush—never an advocate of sanctions—supported the South African government's stance. Despite objections by the ANC, as well as by domestic U.S. supporters of sanctions such as TransAfrica and the Congressional Black Caucus, Bush endorsed the State Department's determination that all political prisoners had been released by signing an executive order lifting U.S. sanctions (*New York Times,* 11 July 1991, A10).

11. Ibid., 3 May 1991, A11.

reform were sincere, thereby satisfying the fifth condition for the lifting of sanctions.[12]

Most international organizations and states duly reopened economic exchange, beginning in late 1990 and continuing into 1991.[13] While de Klerk and other South African officials denied that they had implemented their reforms as part of a contract based on sanctions conditions, they nonetheless expressed their view that the sanctioning countries (specifically the U.S.) now had a moral obligation to lift restrictions.[14]

Against the conventional characterization of an isolationist South African state, these five domestic reforms indicate a compelling coincidence between international demands and government actions. Indeed, South Africa is a "hard case" for the diffusion of an international norm, given the National Party's commitment to white minority rule. Yet preliminary evidence suggests that sanctions succeeded in diffusing a global norm of racial equality in part through changes in external incentives: sanctions increased costs, and the prospect of their removal induced policy change. Thus market power incentives and South African compliance appear to confirm a modified version of neoliberal theory. But the abolition of apartheid cannot be viewed simply in terms of state policy response. Reform entailed restructuring domestic institutions—the internal transformation of the state, a process beyond the boundaries of statecentric theory. The internal effects of international efforts therefore deserve further attention.

12. As in the U.S. deliberations over who were really political prisoners and who "ordinary" criminals, debate flourished over what constituted an "irreversible" commitment to political reforms. Mandela and the ANC wanted international sanctions to be maintained until an election based upon the principle of one-person, one-vote. Their position, however, did not sway predominantly conservative Western leaders.

13. For example, the European Community lifted its sanctions in stages in response to de Klerk's reforms. In December 1990 it rescinded its voluntary ban on investments in South Africa, but members delayed lifting the arms embargo as part of the UN embargo until after the repeal of the legal pillars of apartheid (*New York Times*, 5 February 1991, A3); the EC lifted the rest of its economic restrictions on 15 April 1991 in response to de Klerk's continuing reform efforts (ibid., 16 April 1991, A1). On 11 July 1991, the day after the International Olympic Committee removed its ban against South African sports, the U.S. lifted its sanctions, declaring that de Klerk's movements to abolish apartheid were "irreversible" (ibid., 11 July 1991, A1). In contrast, Britain lifted its sanctions almost immediately after de Klerk's initial reform efforts—specifically Mandela's release—subjecting Thatcher to criticism from diverse sources such as the opposition Labour Party as well as fellow EC members (*The Independent* [London], 13 and 24 February 1990).

14. *New York Times*, 18 June 1991, A8.

LEGITIMATION EFFECTS

Because the elimination of apartheid involved the transformation of domestic politics—in effect the National Party's negotiating itself out of power—it is important to recognize that reform was not simply a state or elite response to external pressure.[15] As comparative studies generally argue, domestic factors also influence a state's foreign policies. In South Africa the ruling National Party firmly controlled the state, but international sanctions created crucial divisions within it and among the white electorate. In addition, various groups were contending for power within a future constitutional system, and international sanctions functioned as a legitimizing force in their search for recognition and representation. All three of the major domestic players in the negotiation process—the National Party, the ANC, and Inkatha—felt the social costs and benefits of international recognition, each in different ways. Thus international sanctions affected the political balance between these three key parties in ways whose complexity is not revealed by studies of coercive capabilities or market incentives.

White solidarity (especially within the National Party) has often been overestimated in political analyses of the effects of international sanctions. As a result, observers have frequently underestimated the importance of the Conservative Party in the 1980s to the reform process.[16] Economic sanctions exacerbated the socioeconomic divisions among whites, thus changing the National Party's support base and strengthening its commitment to reform. Conservative criticism increased in the aftermath of de Klerk's initial reforms. Furthermore, the conservative challenge perpetuated a strong concern over a communist threat, despite the decline and eventual dissolution of the Soviet Union. In response to local elections that indicated growing support for the Con-

15. For an alternative view of socialization that focuses on elite beliefs, see G. John Ikenberry and Charles A. Kupchan, "Socialization and Hegemonic Power," *International Organization* 44 (Summer 1990), 283–315.

16. On the divisions among Afrikaners before de Klerk's ascension, see Graham Leach, *The Afrikaners: Their Last Great Trek* (London: Mandarin, 1989). In its April–May 1989 survey, the Investor Responsibility Research Center attempted to gauge whites' perceptions of international economic sanctions. Its findings substantiate the claim that sanctions were taken seriously by whites in South Africa. See Jan Hofmeyr, *The Impact of Sanctions on White South Africa*, part 2, *Whites' Political Attitudes* (Washington, D.C.: Investor Responsibility Research Center, 1990). On the socioeconomic bases of divisions among Afrikaners before the peak of Western sanctions, see Merle Lipton, *Capitalism and Apartheid: South Africa, 1910–1984* (Aldershot, U.K.: Gower, 1985).

servative Party in areas traditionally loyal to the National Party, de Klerk called for a referendum on the reform process.

The 17 March 1992 all-white referendum on reform is a strong indication of the legitimacy of the National Party reform process. Prior to the vote, speculation ranged broadly over the likely results, illustrating the role of sanctions in white opinion.[17] Debates leading up to the referendum reveal two immediate concerns revolving around sanctions: the threat of renewed international economic restrictions should the referendum fail and, most specifically, renewal of the sports boycott. Newspaper reports reflected views such as: "I decided to vote yes. We need our jobs and we don't need any places closing down, and that is what is going to happen if a no vote wins. Then we'll have just sanctions and we don't want that."[18] Eager to help avert sanctions, white businesses spent over $1 million on proreferendum advertising warning that sanctions would threaten jobs. Newspaper editorials warned of the dangers of a no-vote and gave discounts on proreferendum advertising.[19]

The overwhelming support—68.7 percent of the returns favored the reform referendum—ratified progress toward constitutional negotiations in the face of growing conservative criticism.[20] Postelection commentary also reaffirmed the importance of sanctions: the results were interpreted as a "clear message that [whites] want to become part of the world again rather than live hunkered down in the isolation brought on by apartheid."[21] In particular, the coincidence between the referendum and South Africa's first international cricket match since the lifting of the sports boycott was noted. This preliminary, anecdotal

17. Opinion polls were forbidden (*New York Times*, 18 March 1992, A8).

18. Ibid. Voters on both sides were concerned about violence, but their evaluations of the consequences of the vote varied considerably. Apparently many yes-voters were not optimistic about the future of reform but saw a future under more conservative leadership as even less appealing (see, e.g., ibid., 4 March 1992, A6). Analysis of Afrikaners' attitudes in 1989 confirms a concern over the economic effects of sanctions; worry over the economic implications of black rule persisted as well. See Kate Manzo and Pat McGowan, "Afrikaner Fears and the Politics of Despair: Understanding Change in South Africa," *International Studies Quarterly* 36 (March 1992), 1–24.

19. *New York Times*, 20 March 1992.

20. The referendum specifically asked: "Do you support continuation of the reform process which the State President began on February 2, 1990 and which is aimed at a new constitution through negotiation?" (ibid., 18 March 1992). The Conservatives had vehemently contested the wording, but de Klerk's version prevailed. The referendum lost in only the most conservative areas of the northern Transvaal—and even there de Klerk received 38 percent of the votes (ibid., 26 March 1992).

21. Ibid., 20 March 1992, A7.

evidence indicates the general outlines of a connection between sanctions and support for negotiation on a new constitution. De Klerk succeeded in using the March 1992 vote to legitimize his previous reforms and give himself a mandate to proceed in negotiations with the ANC and other opposition representatives.

The ANC substantially benefitted from international sanctions in two ways. As we have seen in previous chapters, in general international sanctions legitimized opposition to apartheid and, by extension, the ANC demand for universal suffrage. More directly, international organizations including the United Nations, the Organization of African Unity, and the transnational anti-apartheid movement allocated resources to the ANC while in exile, enabling it to remain a viable "government-in-exile" prior to its legalization in 1990. Translating the ANC's external support into internal legitimacy is more complicated. In part it earned credit for domestic political activism of the mid- and late 1980s because its external connections channeled financial support to affiliates such as the United Democratic Front.[22] A less tangible but crucial asset was Mandela's worldwide image. Thus international sanctions and complementary policies allowed the ANC to maintain domestic support until 1990, after which it transformed itself into the predominant domestic opposition political party.

Finally, and most ironically, the third group to gain influence because of international sanctions was Inkatha. Its leader, Chief Mangosuthu Gatsha Buthelezi, was the answer for both foreign and South African conservatives who were searching for a legitimate black representative opposing sanctions. Not only was Buthelezi subsequently toured internationally but, as the "Inkatha-gate" scandal in 1991 revealed, his organization received money from the South African government (in addition to special treatment from police).[23] According to Foreign Minister Pik Botha, the money channeled to Inkatha came from a secret fund used to fight Western sanctions; he had authorized the payments "strictly within the mandate to combat sanctions."[24] In the long term, the Inkatha-gate funding scandal damaged Buthelezi's standing internationally and domestically even though previous government favoritism had been crucial in his rise to prominence (despite his

22. The South African government later prohibited such support, claiming it was subversive. For details on ANC connections to the domestic democratic movement, see Marx, *Lessons of Struggle*. On foreign financing, see Price, *Apartheid State*, p. 233.

23. On South African government support for Inkatha, see Marx, *Lessons of Struggle*, p. 232, and *Facts and Reports* 22 (10 January 1992), 5–6.

24. *New York Times*, 22 July 1992.

proclaimed ignorance of government funding or favoritism). Based in the KwaZulu homeland and Natal Province, Inkatha proved unable to generate nationwide support prior to the 1994 elections.

The relationships outlined here between international sanctions and the abolition of apartheid are preliminary but suggestive. The prospects of renewed sanctions pushed the white electorate to endorse President de Klerk's efforts. Thirty years of international opposition to apartheid had cumulatively strengthened the image of the ANC as the primary representative of the opposition, both at home and abroad. In a further twist of fate, Inkatha at first benefited from sanctions—as the primary black domestic group opposing these restrictions and advocating greater foreign investments—only to be implicated in apartheid later by the discovery of its secret government funding. Thus international sanctions influenced the strength of the domestic actors who in turn negotiated the structure of a postapartheid South Africa based on racial equality, setting the stage for the ANC's electoral triumph in April 1994.

South African elections based on universal suffrage were the product of international, transnational, and domestic pressures that deserve extensive evaluation beyond the scope of this study; nevertheless, this initial evidence of the global dimension of South Africa's domestic transformation demonstrates the importance of international incentives and legitimation processes, not simply of external coercion or interstate bargaining as conventional sanctions analyses suggest. Since evidence from the case of South Africa shows that norm-enforcing sanctions are taken seriously by both senders and targets, our evaluations of sanctions should include criteria that capture the role of norms.

Previous chapters have demonstrated that states implement sanctions not solely because of internationally enforced coercive measures or the mediating role of international institutions. Target states respond to a range of international pressures, including social costs and benefits. If too narrow a focus precludes a more balanced evaluation, however, too broad a list of effects lacks analytical leverage. Rather than simply arguing whether or not sanctions effectively coerce targets, therefore, I have suggested a distinction between coercion, incentive, and legitimation effects.[25] Coercion captures tactical and strategic dimensions of international influence. But threats are not sufficient

25. On the usefulness of subcategories in gauging the utility of sanctions, see Jentleson, *Pipeline Politics*, pp. 31–34.

for explaining power relationships. In addition, incentives based on cost-benefit calculations can induce behavioral change, as neoliberal institutionalists have argued. And furthermore, focusing on legitimation captures a crucial dimension of socialization that is overlooked by conventional behavioral analysis.[26]

Distinguishing between coercion, incentives, and legitimation improves our understanding of senders' choices of sanctions, leading to a focus on the processes by which policy consensus is established. Global opposition to apartheid demonstrated that by expressing censure for noncompliant behavior, even minimal, symbolic sanctions can identify and strengthen international norms. By reinforcing a global norm of racial equality in international arenas, anti-apartheid activists generated multilateral and bilateral sanctions policies. Even though permanent members vetoed coercive economic sanctions in the UN Security Council, various economic and social incentives paved the way for multilateral sanctions in the Commonwealth, the European Community, and the Organization of African Unity. In addition, through domestic mobilization and social transformation, numerous states adopted bilateral sanctions independently of their memberships in international organizations.

The distinction between coercion, incentives, and legitimation also helps us understand the target state's responses to international sanctions. Disaggregating the political effects of sanctions, beyond immediate coercion of the national government, needs to be an important step in evaluating sanctions. If we acknowledge that norm diffusion has a domestic structural component, we begin to see the political and institutional—not solely economic and foreign-policy—consequences of sanctions. Turning the spotlight on racial discrimination in South Africa successfully pressured the target state to comply with international standards; the government abolished apartheid according to the criteria established by the sanctioning organizations and countries. Furthermore, multilateral and bilateral sanctions policies determined recognition of (and allocation of resources to) nonstate actors, notably the African National Congress. The effects of international pressures on South African domestic institutions and actors have yet to be systematically documented, but it is nevertheless clear that the sanctions movement enhanced conditions conducive to a negotiated settlement,

---

26. Steven Lukes calls this the "third dimension" of power; see *Power: A Radical View* (London: Macmillan, 1974).

illustrating the importance of sanctions as a nonmilitary instrument of social rather than coercive power.

If sanctions are to be used as a viable nonmilitary policy, as they increasingly are in various international responses to crises around the world, the implications of international norms for policy need to be better understood. The South African case offers a useful starting point for reevaluating sanctions. Examining the broader effects of social power in international politics leads to a number of questions that should guide empirical examination of the *political* effects of sanctions. Comprehending the various roles of norms in these political processes of coercion, incentives, and legitimation expands our conceptual tools for pursuing this research. Further studies, designed to develop operational standards for evaluating social processes across a wide range of cases, will substantially elucidate the conditions under which sanctions are a useful option for the makers of international policy.

Understanding the implications of norms for policy enhances our understanding of international relations theories as well. Conceiving of sanctions as part of socialization processes, rather than simply as instruments of coercion, reinforces neoliberal and interpretivist critiques of realism. Both states and nonstate actors are motivated and constrained by global norms. Expanding our empirical analyses of sanctions will improve our knowledge of constitutive and regulative norms in a variety of issue areas and under a variety of conditions. Both sanctions analysts and international relations theorists will benefit from the better understanding of social power that this will bring.

CHAPTER TEN

Norms and Identity

As I have argued, the global diffusion of a norm of racial equality motivated domestic, transnational, state, and intergovernmental actors to protest South Africa's system of domestic racial segregation. Even those with substantial interests in maintaining ties with South Africa eventually bent to global pressures demanding sanctions. As a result of these concerted social, economic, and military sanctions, in combination with internal South African mobilization, the National Party government abolished apartheid and conceded to the results of universal-suffrage elections. South Africa has shed its pariah status and is now seeking the rights and recognizing the obligations common to states within the contemporary international system.

This story of the socialization of South Africa is but one example of the force of norms in global politics, yet it highlights important debates in our theorizing about contemporary world politics. By generating multilateral and bilateral sanctions and by promoting racial equality within South Africa, advocates of this global constitutive norm demonstrated that even within the modern state system, weak states and non-state actors have power, a power that is ignored by analyses that focus on military coercion and market incentives alone. Thus both conventional realist and regime theory perspectives offer only partial explanations of the role of norms in world politics.

But rather than simply reinforcing a paradigmatic dichotomy between realist and idealist approaches, the empirical evidence in this study establishes a number of ways we can build on the insights of interpretive and rational-choice institutionalist theories. The socialization of South Africa illustrates two crucial interpretivist theoretical claims (as outlined in chapter 2): that norms constrain states' behavior through reputation and group membership, and that norms constitute states' definitions of their own identities and interests. The first—instrumental—claim suggests further research to explore the role of a social "identity constraint" to complement other rationalist forms of economic cost-benefit calculus. The second—constructivist—claim points to a more substantial additional agenda: research into the social origins of identities and interests. While these two claims about the role of identity in international politics are not totally separable, they do involve different methodologies. Distinguishing these complementary research strategies enables us to move beyond the often acrimonious debates about paradigm dominance, particularly the overstated dichotomy between interpretation and rationality.

RATIONALITY AND IDENTITY CONSTRAINT

This study has engaged debates between social and rational choice theorists over the nature of norms and institutions. But because interpretivists have generally asked a set of complementary, rather than competing, questions about the role of norms, we have had little opportunity to compare the explanatory value of the two approaches. In addition, to the extent that interpretivists initially offered epistemological critiques of structural materialism and methodological individualism without empirically illustrating their relevance for the rationalists' core theoretical concerns, discussion across the paradigmatic divide has been forestalled.[1]

Interpretivists claim that norms, conceived as intersubjective meanings, necessarily preclude unambiguous and objective—quasi-scientific—claims of a neopositivist epistemology. Our languages, for example, determine the concepts we use to understand and explain the world; language also determines how we communicate our individual (subjective) understandings to others. Bias, therefore, is inherently impossible to eliminate, because *all* knowledge is based on socially de-

1. This is not to deny the importance of these metatheoretical concerns; see esp. R. B. J. Walker, *Inside/Outside: International Relations as Political Theory* (Cambridge: Cambridge University Press, 1993), chap. 4. Rather, I am claiming that these positions have explanatory implications as well, as developed in chap. 2 above.

rived assumptions.[2] In practice, this interpretive epistemological claim primarily challenges the *ahistorical* aspects of neorealist and neoliberal analyses. A focus on the concepts of norms and identity, however, enables us to identify many of the social assumptions implicit within both the reality that we analyze and the theories we construct. We can retain historical context without giving up explanatory theory.

Despite their epistemological and ontological differences, both interpretive and rationalist institutionalism claim that norms affect behavior. They differ, however, in the mechanisms of that influence. Rationalists, concentrating on actors' choices, analyze norms as influences on strategic interactions in the pursuit of a given set of interests. Norms, in this view, function as "road maps" that expedite the pursuit of interests and as "focal points" that enhance coordination and resolve the indeterminacy of multiple-equilibria situations.[3] Thus building on economic models, rational choice perspectives emphasize the calculation of (material) costs and benefits. Norms expedite communication and reduce the costs of interaction.

In contrast, interpretive theorists emphasize the constraining effects of legitimation processes and identify norms through prevailing discourses.[4] Norms, in this view, are embedded in social structures. Consequently, actors' definitions of their identities and interests depend on a variable social and historical context. Identity then becomes part of the

2. For a lucid explanation of this broad epistemological claim, see esp. David Couzens Hoy, "Is Hermeneutics Ethnocentric?" in *The Interpretive Turn: Philosophy, Science, and Culture*, ed. David R. Hiley, James F. Bowman, and Richard Shusterman (Ithaca: Cornell University Press, 1991), pp. 155–75, as well as the rest of the volume. I conflate ideology, culture, and knowledge into "norms" throughout this discussion to emphasize the underlying contestable and intersubjective nature of ideas. Knowledge, as well as ideologies and cultures, can be viewed as a set of norms, thus challenging the predominant assumption of objective facts and scientific rules. Tensions between these competing views of knowledge are particularly evident in the literature on epistemic communities, hinting at the relevance of a Foucaultian power perspective. Compare, e.g., Ernst B. Haas, *When Knowledge Is Power: Three Models of Change in International Organizations* (Berkeley: University of California Press, 1990), and Emanuel Adler, "The Emergence of Cooperation: National Epistemic Communities and the International Evolution of the Idea of Arms Control," *International Organization* 46 (Winter 1992), 101–45, with Michel Foucault, *Power/Knowledge: Selected Interviews and Other Writings 1972–1977*, ed. Colin Gordon (New York: Pantheon, 1980).

3. Judith Goldstein and Robert O. Keohane, "Ideas and Foreign Policy: An Analytical Framework," in their edited *Ideas and Foreign Policy: Beliefs, Institutions, and Political Change* (Ithaca: Cornell University Press, 1993), pp. 3–30.

4. See esp. Friedrich Kratochwil and John Gerard Ruggie, "International Organization: A State of the Art on the Art of the State," *International Organization* 40 (Autumn 1986), 753–75, as well as chap. 2 above.

social structure (rather than operating primarily through actors' perceptions and beliefs) that determines behavioral outcome.[5]

In part, identities figure into actors' instrumental cost-benefit calculations. As this study illustrates, under certain circumstances we can safely assume the identities and interests of various actors, whereupon we can analyze some but not all of their actions in material terms. Sometimes, however, actors include social costs, such as reputation and group membership, in their calculations. Britain, for example, compromised on its sanctions policy in reaction to social pressures that had no substantial material threats attached. Within a number of states, including the United States and Zimbabwe, conservatives compromised their economic interests in order to affirm their support for racial equality at home and in South Africa. By arguing that this identity affirmation, the desire to demonstrate a nonracist identity, functions as one component of cost and benefit calculation, we can compare rationalist and interpretivist claims. "Identity constraint" thus offers one avenue for bridging the agent-structure gap in these two institutionalisms.[6]

Additional empirical studies need to generate much broader evidence before we can evaluate the strength of these contrasting claims. Meanwhile, South Africa's reaction to international pressures, as analyzed in chapter 9, offers preliminary evidence of the complex ways in which identity constraint operates. At the level of interstate interaction, multilateral and bilateral conditions for legitimacy gave the South African government incentives to eliminate apartheid: doing so would end sanctions. At the domestic level as well, both social and economic sanctions appear to have convinced the white electorate that the benefits of

5. Because of these noninstrumental effects, norms do not fit easily into conventional behavioral conceptions of power and causality. But the more narrowly external constraints limit the range of policy choice, the more closely such constraint resembles motivational cause. To the extent that structures limit the range of actors' choices, at the most extreme to "fight or die" (the neorealist claim), we can consider them to cause behavior. See Steven Lukes's introduction to *Power*, ed. Steven Lukes (Oxford: Basil Blackwell, 1986), pp. 1–18, as well as Kratochwil and Ruggie, "International Organization."

6. Compare esp. Alexander Wendt, "Anarchy Is What States Make of It: The Social Construction of Power Politics," *International Organization* 46 (Spring 1992), pp. 391–425, and Arthur A. Stein, *Why Nations Cooperate: Circumstance and Choice in International Relations* (Ithaca: Cornell University Press, 1990), chap. 4. I therefore reject the pervasive dichotomy that characterizes "interpretation" as solely about "understanding," versus social science theories about "explaining." On its implications for international relations theories, see Martin Hollis and Steve Smith, *Explaining and Understanding International Relations* (Oxford: Clarendon Press, 1990), and more generally Daniel C. Little, *Varieties of Social Explanation: An Introduction to the Philosophy of Social Science* (Boulder, Colo.: Westview Press, 1991).

reform (including the resumption of international sporting contacts in addition to normal trade relations) outweighed the costs to them of majority rule. Neither Afrikaner leaders nor the white electorate, however, needed to be converted to a sincere belief in racial equality to eliminate the apartheid system. White South Africans were induced— rather than coerced—to reform by a combination of material and social incentives.

Thus the legitimation of certain goals and means partially defines costs but cannot predict more than a range of likely choices. With methodologies appropriate to intersubjective meanings, therefore, we can analyze global norms as we do other structural components. Adding an identity component to constraint lets us combine agent perspectives with structural analysis and so furthers attempts among choice-theorists to contextualize rationality.[7] Particularly importantly, given the prevalence of an assumption among social scientists that Africans are "traditional" and therefore somehow nonrational or irrational, rationalist perspectives help us understand that Pan-Africanists calculated the costs and benefits of advocating racial equality. Because of the profound importance of eliminating racism, they chose to forego economic gains and absorb security costs in their opposition to South Africa.[8]

As I argued in detail in chapter 2, the concepts of reputation and community offer good methodological tools for pursuing this para-digm-bridging type of research into how and why—and not simply whether—norms matter. In addition, focusing on identity constraint demonstrates that an interpretive theory is not simply an anti-behavioralist methodology or antipositivist epistemology. Acknowledging the role of identity constraint, however, introduces a second set of questions, about the origins of identity and its relationship to interests.

SOCIAL CONSTRUCTION OF IDENTITY

To claim that states are socialized into the international system presumes a conception of identity. As a starting point for analysis, I have

7. See Eileen Crumm, "Economic Incentives in International Politics" (manuscript, University of Southern California); also Hollis and Smith, *Explaining and Understanding*, chap. 7.

8. Unfortunately, analysts' social assumptions frequently do bias their theories, and racism in particular remains uncomfortably linked to "scientific" knowledge as well as social practice. See esp. Stephen Jay Gould, *The Mismeasure of Man* (New York: Norton, 1981). On the rationality of Africans, see esp. Kwame Anthony Appiah, *In My Father's House: Africa in the Philosophy of Culture* (New York: Oxford University Press, 1992).

supposed three dimensions of South Africa's international identity: global/Western, European/colonial, and African. This study was designed to assess how a strengthened norm of racial equality transformed these identities and the relationships between actors within identity communities, not to explain the origin of that norm or of South Africa's initial identity. But the issue of its identity raises broader questions about the past and future of South African international relations. Comparing norms across different historical periods also brings up more abstract issues concerning the nature of international systems and the international politics of (state) identity.

For example, an analysis of the origins and transformation of apartheid demonstrates that the norm of racial equality plays a constitutive role because "race" is an identity-defining concept (although the criteria used in identifying racial divisions vary across periods and societies). A political and social doctrine based on racial hierarchies, such as South African apartheid, distinguishes biological differences between groups of people (Whites, Coloureds, Asians, and Africans, in this case) that underpin institutions that reinforce social hierarchies.[9] The removal of South Africa's race classification law, the Population Registration Act, heralded the demise of the apartheid system because all other segregation laws depended on this legal basis for distinguishing racial groups. Once South Africa adopted a system based on racial equality as a political rather than economic right, its international isolation ended. Thus international sanctions succeeded in promoting a particular definition of a democratic, nonracial South Africa.

Furthermore, since the white minority government of the early 1990s responded to international socialization pressures, we must question whether the racist ideology of apartheid itself originated as a domestic, rather than international or transnational, construction. Despite its reputation as an isolationist state, South Africa has always been influenced by international social forces. Many analysts have observed over the years that apartheid merely formalized racist views already

9. The distinction between Whites, Coloureds, and Blacks in southern Africa contrasts with a dichotomy between whites and blacks prevalent in the United States. In addition, among South African opponents of apartheid, many Coloureds and Asians identified themselves as Black in rejection of official categorizations, which divided resistance. Thus while apartheid justified social divisions biologically, resistance politics illustrates the social construction of identity. See Julie Fredrickse, *The Unbreakable Thread: Non-Racialism in South Africa* (Bloomington: Indiana University Press, 1990), and Anthony W. Marx, *Lessons of Struggle: South African Internal Opposition, 1960–1990* (New York: Oxford University Press, 1992).

dominant among whites, Anglo as well as Afrikaner, and that these views echoed those dominant among European colonial powers. Furthermore, apartheid ideologists relied on a global norm of self-determination in attempting to legitimize "separate development" (apartheid). The creation of "independent" homelands resembled the decolonization process of the 1960s, and conservative Afrikaners still invoke self-determination in their demands for a separate white state today.

Let us extrapolate from the South African example. These identities do not simply correspond to sovereign states, evolving autonomously in isolation from other actors. The international and transnational aspects of South African identity, which I have explored here only in terms of race, illustrate fundamental tensions between statecentric and transnational social forces. Transnational social movements (including the anti-apartheid movement as well as missionary societies in the colonial era and a continual flow of immigrants around the globe) are all relevant to our theorizing about international and domestic transformations.[10] Indeed, for South Africa as for other former British colonies, sovereignty within the Commonwealth evolved gradually while autonomous boundaries remained unclear in practice.

Nor will the new, nonracial South Africa evolve in isolation. Some international pressures, such as membership in the United Nations and the International Monetary Fund, reaffirm statecentric sovereign identities (though not necessarily sovereign autonomy). Other memberships, such as in the Commonwealth and OAU, promote broader transnational and collective commitments. As Zimbabwe discovered, former white minority–ruled states face numerous, often incompatible demands from advocates of economic nationalism on the one hand and African solidarity on the other. How the new South Africa reconciles similar tensions will depend in part on how it defines national security. But unlike Zimbabwe, South Africa has no obvious, racially defined regional enemies, making the prospects for peace and prosperity in the region brighter than in 1980.[11] South Africa's new nonracial identity may contribute toward a community identity that mitigates the differ-

10. For similar analyses of transnational social movements, see Franke Wilmer, *The Indigenous Voice in World Politics: Since Time Immemorial* (Newbury Park, Cal.: Sage, 1993), and Daniel Thomas, "International Norms and Political Change: The Helsinki Accords and the Decline of Communism, 1972–1989" (Ph.D. diss., Cornell University, in progress).

11. On the social construction of threat and security, see David Campbell, *Writing Security: United States Foreign Policy and the Politics of Identity* (Minneapolis: University of Minnesota Press, 1992), and for the Zimbabwe comparison, see chap. 8 above.

ent security interests that are inherent in sovereign identities. Alternatively, internal ethnic divisions may undermine African and sovereign identities.[12]

The evolution of South African foreign and domestic relations illustrates the importance of avoiding rigid distinctions between international anarchy and domestic society in analyzing state identities. Rather, we should recognize elements of society in the international system and also elements of anarchy in domestic politics. States and state identities are part of a broader category of political communities that are subject to global processes.[13] From this characterization of states as social groups or political communities, we can put the formation of states in historical context and understand the content of identities. Prevailing norms identify one form of a constitutive, rather than solely instrumental, action. By explaining the role that norms play in defining identities and interests, interpretive theory offers an expanded conceptualization of world politics that corresponds to its ontological assumption that agents and structures reconstitute each other.

I began this study by asking how widespread global cooperation—collective action against apartheid—could be possible in a world of states rationally pursuing their material interests. The subsequent empirical analyses of international organizations and states demonstrated how global constitutive norms and legitimation processes challenge the realist and neoliberal anarchy assumption, even while reaffirming the role of states as actors. Global authority structures can be transnational and decentralized; they need not function like domestic governments on a supranational scale.

By stressing race—particularly conflicts between racial equality and racial superiority—this study has also pointed to the importance of analyzing constitutive norms not only for understanding why global actors take particular actions but also for identifying biases in our own choice of important political questions. Because constitutive norms such as racial equality and the broader social structures in which they

12. Indeed, we could apply international relations theories to South Africa's internal fragmentation. Negotiations for the new federal constitution bear striking similarities to regime theory expectations. For a preliminary analysis along these lines, see Donald L. Horowitz, *A Democratic South Africa? Constitutional Engineering in a Divided Society* (Berkeley: University of California Press, 1991).

13. See esp. Walker, *Inside/Outside;* also compare Alexander Wendt "Collective Identity Formation and the International State," *American Political Science Review* 88 (June 1994), 384–96.

are embedded are not visible simply through behavioral analyses, we often unduly narrow our range of legitimate questions by adopting conventional research agendas. This is not to say that traditional questions of war and trade are unimportant but that many other questions are also crucial if we want to understand and influence the world in which we live. Conventional international relations theorists, for example, have studied Africa primarily as a passive arena for rivalries among great powers. But the history of decolonization, like that of the anti-apartheid movement, demonstrates the power of weak and nonstate actors to transform both global norms and the distribution of social power in the international system. If actors define their own identities and interests in transnational rather than territorial terms, our theories should reflect this reality.

The abolition of apartheid, then, marks a substantial transformation for the continent that should lead analysts—of both African and global politics—to rethink African identity and the continent's position in world politics. South Africa's metamorphosis into a nonracial democracy may indeed succeed past the initial constitution-writing stage, but there are no guarantees that racism has been eliminated either locally or globally, and nationalism and economic conflict simmer as well. Peaceful transformation is not inevitable, but it is possible.

Index

African-American Institute, 96
African Liberation Committee (of the
OAU), 78, 79
African National Congress (ANC)
  and British colonialism, 113
  and British policies, 118, 119, 124
  and Commonwealth policies, 122
  and diplomatic sanctions, 49
  and incentive effects, 155
  international aid to, 161
  and South African destabilization, 85,
    86
  and South African domestic reform,
    155, 156, 157–58, 159, 161
  unbanning of, 156
  and U.S. policies, 108, 110
  and Zimbabwean policies, 143
African states
  economic sanctions, 5n
  and Rhodesian independence conflict,
    61, 62, 76
  and United Nations, 9, 46, 54
  See also Decolonization era; Frontline
    States; Organization of African Unity;
    Pan-Africanist perspective; South Afri-
    can regional destabilization; Zimba-
    bwe
African Studies Association, 96
Algeria, 75
Altruism, 13
American Committee on Africa, 96

American Negro Leadership Conference
  on Africa, 96
American Society of African Culture, 96
Anglo-Boer war, 113
Angola, 51, 65, 75, 79
  international aid to, 84n
  South African defeat, 89
  U.S. policies, 107
  See also Frontline States; South African
    regional destabilization
Anti-apartheid movement
  and British policies, 11, 113–16, 118n
  and Commonwealth policies, 56
  international aid, 53, 161
  and international institutions, 24
  and OAU, 89, 90
  and racial equality norm, 6, 17
  and United Nations, 40, 53
  U.S. grassroots movement, 94, 95–100
  See also specific groups and topics
Apartheid
  and capitalism, 7–8
  construction of, 170–71
  defined, 3n
  inherent violence of, 108
  institutionalization of, 43, 44
  justifications for, 4, 42, 47
  and race classification, 170
  varied responses to, 33–35
  See also specific topics
Arms embargoes. See Military sanctions

175

Cornell Studies in Political Economy

EDITED BY PETER J. KATZENSTEIN

About the Author

Susan D. Stewart is a professor of sociology at Iowa State University. She is author or co-author of several books including *Co-Sleeping: Parents, Children, and Musical Beds*, *Marriages, Families, and Relationships*, *Brave New Stepfamilies*, and *Multicultural Stepfamilies*. Her research focuses on gender, family diversity, parenting, and children and adults' physical, social, and emotional health. She has published articles on a range of topics in leading peer-reviewed journals such as *Journal of Marriage and Families*, *Journal of Family Issues*, *Demography*, and *Journal of Gynecology and Women's Health*. Dr. Stewart resides in Ames, Iowa with her husband, daughter, and three cats.